GROWN UP BOX OF TOYS

LORRAINE MICHELE

*Dedicated to Zach, my amazing son.
From day one, you've made parenting a joy.
You are truly, the best.*

Contents

Introduction 7

1. DOLLS AND TEDDIES - For Your Child
Self-Esteem 9
Eight Steps for Building your Child's Self-Esteem 11
For You
Are you FOR or AGAINST you? 16
Nine Keys to Unlocking your own Positive Self-Esteem 17
Famous Last Words 21

2. STICKERS - For Your Child
Labelling 23
For You
Self-Talk - Your Own Inner Sticker 25
So what is Self-Talk? 25
Famous Last Words 31

3. SKIPPING ROPES - For Your Child
Routines 33
Three Simple Suggestions 34
Why Not? 36
For You
Change 37
Charting your own Course 37
Famous Last Words 41

4. BOOKS - For Your Child
Reading 42
For You
Education 45
Famous Last Words 50

5. BUBBLES, BALLOONS and KITES - For Your Child
Shooting for the Moon 52
For You
Wishes, Dreams and Goals 54
Four Tips for following your Star 59

Famous Last Words   63

6. KITCHENS and COOKERS - For Your Child
Healthy Eating   65
The Fabulous Four   68
For You
Weight Loss   70
The Inside Skinny – Five Tips   71
Exercise – Getting a jump on your Day   74
Famous Last Words   76

7. TEA SETS - For Your Child
Manners   77
Reaping what they Sow   81
For You
Kindness   83
Famous Last Words   86

8. CRAYONS and PAINTS - For Your Child
Appreciating Beauty   88
For You
Beauty Within   90
Ten Steps for Improving your Self-Confidence   93
Famous Last Words   97

9. BUILDING BLOCKS - For Your Child
The Value of Money   99
Coins and Fairy Godmothers   100
For You
Financial Freedom   101
Nine Simple ways to Economize   102
Famous Last Words   106

10. WENDYHOUSE - For Your Child
Tantrums and Bullies   107
The Dreaded Temper Tantrum   108
Signs of Bullying   112
Effective Steps   113

For You
Bullying, Arguments and Conflicts   115
Disagreements are Natural   116
Fighting Fair – 5 Ground Rules   118
Famous Last Words   120

11. DRESSING UP - For Your Child
Finding Themselves   122
For You
Visualization   124
Scripting your own Life   125
Seeing with the Mind's Eye   125
The Art of Visualization - Wealth, Happiness and Success   126
Famous Last Words   132

12. JIGSAWS - For Your Child
Acceptance   134
Cultivating Tolerance in your Kids   135
For You
Tolerance   138
Standing up for Yourself   139
Famous Last Words   143

13. ABACUS - For Your Child
Growing up too Fast   145
Allow your child to enjoy being a Kid   147
For You
Procrastination   149
Stop procrastinating NOW!   150
Living for the Moment   151
Famous Last Words   153

Acknowledgements   154

*"The best way to make children good,
is to make them happy."*
Oscar Wilde - Author and Poet

Introduction

Parenting is one of the most magnificent, rewarding and daunting occupations many adults will ever experience, yet frequently, when we find ourselves immersed in our new full-time career, parents feel utterly unqualified. For the majority, it's a case of learning as you go, trusting that as we love and nurture our children, we perform the best possible job. A key element of that job is to ensure our child's happiness, education and development.

According to child psychotherapists, infant language specialists and scientists, playing with toys not only provides a great deal of fun but is also a vital part of that development. It follows then, that if we used those same toys as a metaphor for both our children's and our own lives, a wealth of information could be gleaned.

It was in pursuit of this idea, that this book was created.

In **'Dolls & Teddies'**, we discover the impact of a positive or negative Self-esteem. **'Stickers'** demonstrate how labels can last forever and the importance of 'Self-talk', our own inner sticker. **'Dressing Up'** covers visualization. **'Jigsaws'** highlights tolerance both in our children and ourselves. **'Wendy House'** focuses on tantrums, bullying and conflicts. **'Tea Sets'** emphasize manners and kindness. **'Bubbles, Balloons & Kites'** shows why it's imperative for children to dream and why we, as parents, should make our *own* dreams a reality. **'Kitchens & Cookers'** covers the basics of eating right and the sensible way to lose weight. From **'Skipping Ropes'** we learn the importance of routines but also of change.

Be it **'Books'** an **'Abacus'** **'Building Blocks'** or **'Crayons & Paints'** this book offers a fresh and inspiring way of delivering empowering messages to parents, about both their children *and* themselves. I hope you enjoy.

*"Toys are children's words
and play is their language."
Garry L Landreth – Founder of the Centre
for Play Therapy*

Chapter 1 – DOLLS AND TEDDIES

Part 1 - For Your Child

SELF-ESTEEM

*"We just need to be kinder to ourselves.
If we treated ourselves the way
we treated our best friend, can you imagine
how much better off we would be."*
Meghan - Duchess of Sussex

Ever noticed how tenderly a child treats his or her favorite teddy or doll, as though it were the most precious possession in the world. Apart from you and their loved ones, it most probably is. Often children can't even sleep without them, for dolls and teddies command a special place in their hearts and worlds that nothing else can replace. After having all this love and attention lavished on them, believe me, if those teddies and dolls were real, they would not only feel like the most special creatures in the world but their self-esteem would be sky high.

But what is **Self- Esteem** and why is it so important? Psychologists define self-esteem as a positive or negative orientation towards one's self and one's value. Self-esteem encompasses a whole variety of beliefs, including the appraisal of one's appearance, emotions, self-respect, self-assurance, beliefs and behaviors. A healthy self-esteem means having confidence in one's own worth and pride in one's abilities.

When children feel totally loved and secure, it enables them to feel good about themselves and to face their futures with confidence. These kids have great self-esteem, communicate well, are optimistic and welcome new challenges. For them, the sun shines not only on the outside but on the inside too. It's vital therefore as parents that we do everything we can, to build up our child's positive self–esteem, for how children value themselves, affects not only their happiness but every aspect of their future. Putting it bluntly, a child simply cannot enjoy a fulfilling and wonderful life without it. A healthy self-image is one of the greatest gifts any parent can bestow on a child, and it starts from the day they are born, for a parent's love and care determines how that child will mature.

Predictably the opposite is also true, for if a child has been yelled at, abused, teased or even bullied, he or she is going to feel incredibly insecure about themselves, resulting in a very low self-esteem. These insecurities can manifest themselves in a variety of negative ways. Youngsters may feel anxious, detached and angry; often submitting to peer pressure, especially from friends. They may be haunted by self-criticism, such as they're 'stupid' or 'no good'. An insecure child can be easily swayed, be reluctant to try new things, or simply give up too easily when struggling with a new task or challenge, then turn around and blame others for their failures. These unhappy kids frequently feel inadequate, pessimistic and sad, and no child ever deserves to feel this way about themselves, or any aspect of their life.

If these words sound familiar and you're concerned, in any way about your child's self-image, act today, for the longer a child stews in own their destructive thoughts, the greater the chance they have of setting themselves up for future failure and sabotaging their entire life, instead of living it gloriously to the full.

Eight Steps for Building Your Child's Self-Esteem
Following are eight simple steps parents can implement, to help develop their youngster's positive self-esteem.

Step 1 - Love Your Child Unconditionally
Obvious though it may seem, it sometimes needs to be said. Every parent should cherish their child for the remarkable little person he or she is. Be generous with your affection, give cuddles and kisses as a matter of course. Tell your child how much you love them and how proud and delighted you are to be their parent and to raise them. Praise your kids, encouraging them on *all* their endeavors, not just their achievements. Praise isn't to be trotted out merely as a reward for winning or a good deed, but for all their effort and their enthusiasm. Your love will go a long way to creating that all important positive self-image.

Step 2 - Spend Time with Your Children
How can a child possibly feel special if he's constantly battling for your attention? Have fun together and be his friend. Switch off that Smartphone or IPad, take your eyes off the computer or TV and chat together, whether it's at home sharing tea and biscuits, walking home from school, or over dinner. Ask him about his day, encourage him to open up, sharing not only his experi-

ences, but also his feelings and ideas. Show him you truly care, that you're interested and that you enjoy his company.

Step 3 - Talk Nice

> *"Your kids require you most of all to love them for who they are, not to spend your whole time trying to correct them."*
> Bill Ayers - Elementary Education Theorist

Watch how you speak to your child, you know yourself, words really can cut deep. Criticizing or calling a child a "moron" or "lazy" hurts. Warning them to "shut up" or else, certainly doesn't induce good behavior, neither do threats. Avoid comments that are harsh, accusing or judgmental. Belittling your child or their accomplishments is not only unkind but mean. To develop a positive self-image, kids have to feel good about themselves, derogatory words or strident name calling, instantly destroys that. Speak to them as a little person not just a child, according them the same amount of respect and kindness that you in turn would desire, for the way you talk to your children today, will undoubtedly be the way they speak to you tomorrow.

Step 4 - Teach Responsibility

Whenever possible, allow your child to make his or her decisions. They may seem small, even insignificant choices to you, such as whether a toddler would prefer an apple or pear, or even which t-shirt to wear but to your child they are vitally important, underpinning both value and confidence in their own decisions. When you ask your child to help you with a somewhat mundane chore, such as putting away their toys, tack on "there's a good boy/girl" at the end. Not only will this re-enforce what you've asked for, in a positive way, but inevitably your child will happily comply and complete the task. Kind words can make even the littlest chest swell with pride.

Step 5 - Listen to Your Kids

> *"What lies behind us and what lies ahead of us are tiny matters, compared to what lives within us."*
> Ralph Waldo Emerson - Essayist & Poet

Encourage your kids to be honest, sharing their own opinions without fear of recrimination or embarrassment, whether you agree with their sentiments or not. To ride rough shod over them is not acceptable, for if you trample over or condemn their views, one day your kids will simply stop sharing them with you, and a whole lot more besides. Allow children to be free and to air their thoughts. Teach them the value of their own judgment and how to listen and express themselves, while respecting other people's point of view.

If your kids have a problem, empathize and relate some of your own similar experiences, including the daft and crazy things you did when you were young, then try to figure out a solution between you. Small children may be naive about the dangers of life but if you listen, even when they're very young, children can frequently astound, with their own unique gems of wisdom.

Step 6 - Never Compare Siblings

Comparing siblings either favorably or unfavorably is a huge mistake, as one of them will inevitably lose out. Every child is unique and should be treated accordingly. Celebrate each one's differing personality, talents and abilities, allowing them to develop in their own time and at their own pace. If your child takes a little longer to learn a new skill than their sibling, so what, you know they'll get there in the end. Imagine what a dull world it would be, if every child or human being were identical. If sibling rivalry is rife, encourage the older child to help a younger one with an activity, such as reading or maybe even sharing a game. Bonding together can truly work wonders.

Step 7 - Let Them Err
We all make mistakes, including me, you and the rest of the world, it's part of life. Help your child to become their own best friend and to learn to laugh at their mistakes. Children can often try their best and still have difficulty. If they're not given the chance or are too afraid to fail, they will never learn to succeed, and with each success comes an even better self-esteem. After all, it's from our failures and mistakes that we learn to become successful.

Step 8 - Teach Them to Assert Themselves
Standing up for themselves and what they believe in, without hurting or alienating others, is a huge badge of confidence. Show your child how to be polite and handle different situations, so they can learn by your example. If another child is being pushy towards them, perhaps taking your child's sweets or toys, tell the child in a gentle but firm way that taking sweets is not the fair thing to do and that the sweets are to be shared. Teaching your child to be assertive will boost her confidence in a variety of ways, including making new friends and raising her hand at school, when she knows or tries to answer a question.

When you are being assertive, especially in front of your child, i.e. returning damaged merchandise to a less than helpful shop assistant, be as courteous and forthright as you can. Don't fall back on the kind of behavior you previously discouraged. Avoid being a hypocrite or confusing your child, by preaching one thing whilst doing another.

*"Children have never been very good
at listening to their elders
but they have never failed to imitate them."*
James Arthur Baldwin - Essayist Playwright & Novelist

Though all these steps are essential for building your child's positive self-esteem, their greatest influence in all the world is of course *you*. Kids scrutinize their parents and their behavior like hawks and for better or worse, parents affect their offspring more than they could possibly imagine.

If you are negative, overly harsh or excessively critical of yourself, your kids will pick up on it big time and eventually begin to copy you. In order for your children to feel happy about themselves, *you've* got to feel happy about you. After all, you are their greatest role model. So take a moment and ask yourself....

How do you feel about *you*?

Part 2 – FOR YOU

ARE YOU FOR OR AGAINST YOU?

"Of all the judgments you make in life, none is as important as the one you make about yourself."
Nathaniel Brandon - Psychologist

Step back and take stock of yourself and your life. When you look in the mirror, are you proud of the person who stares back? Are you happy? Do you like yourself, are you utilizing all your talents and abilities? Are you making the most of life…are you making the most of you?

If you answered 'No' to any of the above, maybe it's time you questioned your own self-esteem, for a healthy self-image could literally transform your life. But first you must decide if you are for or against you, for in life, so many people are often their own worst enemy. As Eleanor Roosevelt, wife of President Roosevelt rightly declared:

*"No one can make you feel inferior
without your consent."*

If you've been dwelling in, or reliving the past and its mistakes, realize that it's time to change and start living in the now, after all, that is the only guaranteed time we have. From today, try the following for just one month, you'll be astounded at how quickly your self-image will grow and how amazing you'll begin to feel.

Nine Keys – To Unlocking Your Own Positive Self-Esteem

Key 1 – Become your own Cheer-Leader - Believe in You
If you don't, who will? Negative self-esteem is merely an opinion not a fact, and as such, can very easily be changed. Like everything else, a positive self-esteem starts with a simple decision. Sit down right now and list ten things you like about yourself, even if it takes a whole hour! Think about your accomplishments, your skills, your numerous character traits. Are you perceptive, funny, intelligent, adventurous, tenacious, friendly or kind? What have you achieved? Don't say nothing because I guarantee you have, maybe your skills have simply been overlooked. Keep your list handy and every day add one new thing you either like about yourself or have achieved that day. In four short weeks, you'll have so many positive statements, your self-esteem will already be on the rise.

Key 2 – Be Your Own Best Friend - As Oscar Wilde said *"To love oneself is the beginning of a lifelong romance."* From today, respect, love and nurture yourself unequivocally, for life really is as good as your relationship with yourself. We love to hear charitable words from others but inside, if you just listen, you've a zillion kind words available for yourself. Use them. If you don't love yourself, it'll be almost impossible to love others.

Key 3 – Be True to Yourself
If your instincts alert you that something is wrong, listen to them. Instincts or your intuition rarely lie and are very often nature's warning system against harm. If your behavior is causing you to feel guilty or bad, ask yourself, why? Follow and trust your intuition, for it will never let you down. You may choose to hide your feelings from someone else, but you can never hide them from yourself.

Key 4 – Be Open-Minded
Accept weakness both in others and in yourself. It's okay to be vulnerable, it's what makes us human and imperfections are often very endearing. If you stop nitpicking at others, you'll be more inclined to let up on yourself. If someone close criticizes you, don't feel crushed. If it's a fair comment, learn by it. If not, simply discard it.

Key 5 – Make Time for You
So often women selflessly put themselves last, denying themselves any time or space, allowing everyone else's needs to take priority; understandable when you are caring for children, the family or elderly or infirm relatives, besides running the home and probably working too. But constantly prioritizing others needs and putting them permanently top of the list, leaves you feeling angry, frustrated, exhausted and resentful towards everything and everybody, till in the end you literally explode.

Though your actions are prompted out of love and concern for other's welfare, we all need time, even if it is only twenty minutes a day. Allow yourself to be pampered without feeling guilty or inadequate, for you deserve to be indulged as much as anyone. Take a moment to unwind and recharge your batteries, your family and you will certainly reap the benefits. Relax in a warm scented bubble bath, curl up with a good book or magazine, listen to a great CD, indulge in a heavenly 15 min nap or simply close your eyes and do nothing, you'll feel so much more energized and enthused. Maybe you'll acknowledge for the first time, that you are also important, and as such need a little space. Once you do, other people will recognize it too and stop taking you for granted, treating you with the proper respect, love and care that you deserve. Despite what anyone says, nobody likes a martyr. As the lovely Helen Mirren declares in her L'Oréal Ad "...*you're worth it.*"

Key 6 – Set Goals

> *"The whole point of being alive, is to evolve into the complete person you were intended to be."*
> *Oprah Winfrey - U.S. Television Media Mogul & Philanthropist*

Be adventurous and try new things. What have you always secretly longed to do or be? Decide exactly what you desire out of life and become the person you've always wanted to be. Don't think that when you stop school or college, learning automatically stops, it doesn't, in fact it could be just the beginning. Believe wholeheartedly in your abilities as you journey towards a happier and more fulfilling future.

Key 7 – Forgive Yourself
Especially when you've messed up or maybe just not accomplished what you hoped. Perhaps you dieted for a week then went off it big time, culminating in a binge. Don't beat yourself up. Over eating is nothing compared to the orgy of self-recrimination you'll experience. To err is human. Realize that with the best of intentions, we all make mistakes. Be smart, learn from them, then get back in the saddle and get on with it. Prove to yourself, you can succeed.

Key 8 – Accept Compliments Gracefully
When someone pays you a compliment, receive it gracefully with a simple smile and a 'thank you'. Don't immediately bat it away with another compliment for them, or make some deroga-

tory statement about yourself, to hide your embarrassment; savor the compliment but save yours for a more appropriate time. When you pay it, you'll be amazed at how good it makes you feel.

Key 9 – Don't Compare Yourself
It's futile, depressing and a complete waste of time and women are certainly the guiltiest, yet another sign of female insecurity. Take a leaf from the guys, don't do it.

Why is it that women, even in the 21st century, continually compare themselves to every other female? Stop striving to be like someone else, instead strive to be the very best, *you*. Judging yourself negatively by superhuman standards is yet another form of abuse, and many who do, end up frustrated or discouraged, especially when comparing oneself against stick-thin models or jaw dropping movie stars. Be aware that an inordinate amount of time and money is spent on maintaining those glamorous looks and magazine photos are invariably air-brushed to within an inch of their lives. There will always be slimmer, taller, smarter, prettier women, but so what? They are not you and do not have your innate essence or qualities.

Instead of likening yourself to someone else, revel in being you. Accept yourself for who you are and celebrate your uniqueness. You are not the sum total of your looks but all your other wonderful qualities. Make the most of them. Be proud of who you are. After all, you will never be as good at being someone else, as you will, at being *you*, for you are the most perfect you, anyone could ever be.

Value and care for yourself. Eat healthily, get adequate sleep, exercise regularly and make the most of your appearance. Trust me, armed with that new confidence, you will soon be the one, turning heads.

As your self-esteem grows, reward yourself for all your accomplishments and success. Enjoy them. Enjoy you. Pretty soon, just like those kids, the sun will be shinning on the *inside* for you too.

FAMOUS LAST WORDS

For Your Child

*"The child must know that he is a miracle
that since the beginning of the world,
there hasn't been, and until the end of the
world, there will not be another child like him."*
Pablo Casals - Spanish/Musician Conductor

*"One of the most important things
you can say to your child,
'I believe in you.'"*
Anon

*"There can be no keener revelation of a society's soul,
than the way in which it treats its children."*
Nelson Mandela - Former President of South Africa

*"The most precious jewels you'll ever have around your neck
are the arms of your children."*
Anon

For You

*"I think the most important thing for me
is to be true to yourself.
It sounds like a simple thing to do but it's not.
Belief in one's self and knowing who you are –
that's the foundation for everything great."*
Jay Zee - Rapper & Record Producer

*"You, yourself as much as anybody in the entire universe,
deserve your love and affection."*
Buddha – Religious Leader

*"If your self-esteem really depends on how you look, you're always going to be insecure…
What you do and say, is so much more important than how you look."*
Portia De Rossi Actress - Model & Philanthropist

"The important thing is to realize that no matter what people's opinions may be, they're only just that – people's opinions. You have to believe in your heart what you know to be true about yourself. And let that be that."
Mary J Blige – Singer, Songwriter & Actress

"You can't control how other people see you or think of you. But you have to be comfortable with that."
Helen Mirren – Stage, TV & Film Actress

"I've finally stopped running away from myself. Who else is there better to be?"
Goldie Hawn – Actress, Director & Producer

Chapter 2 – STICKERS

Part 1 - For Your Child

LABELLING

"Affirming words from moms and dads are like light switches. Speak a word of affirmation at the right moment in a child's life and it's like lighting up a whole roomful of possibilities."
Gary Smalley - Family Counselor & Author

Children love receiving a complimentary sticker telling them they are 'super', 'brilliant', a 'star' or maybe even a message of congratulations. A sticker shows they've been good, kind or clever and is usually given as a reward for something positive. Besides helping kids achieve things, stickers validate how proud we are of them, how pleased they should be with themselves.

"What a child doesn't receive, he can seldom later give."
P.D. James - Novelist

No matter what the children's rhyme may say, there's a reason we don't give children abusive stickers with scathing or degrading names. Why? Because quite simply, stickers *stick*. Naturally it's a parent's duty and responsibility to guide and correct our kids, but name-calling or labelling children as "fat "or "bad" sends kids a very strong negative message about themselves. The more they hear it, the more likely they are to start believing it and ultimately, the more they'll grow into it, even though they weren't originally. Those humiliating and destructive beliefs can last a lifetime, for you give your child no way of ever shaking or rectifying that label. Like the old drip, drip, torture proves, tell someone something enough times and pretty soon they'll begin to believe it, even if it's a lie. Sadly, those stickers or derogatory labels can shadow your child around in their minds, forever.

From now on, make a point of accentuating only the positive in your child. Call them good names, names you can both be proud of, labels that they can willingly and happily grow into. Tell them how creative, brave, wonderful, fun and bright they are. Little words can have a huge impact.

Part 2 – FOR YOU

SELF-TALK - YOUR OWN INNER STICKER

"The most important key to permanent enhancement of self-esteem is the practice of positive self-talk."
Denis Waitley - Writer & Keynote Speaker

"Every waking moment we talk to ourselves about the things we experience, our self-talk, the thoughts we communicate to ourselves, in turn control the way we feel and act."
John Lembo – Author

So what is Self-Talk?

Self-talk is the constant internal dialogue we have with ourselves, the words we use and the thoughts we have. Self-talk is what creates our feelings, our reality and our general outlook in life. Self-talk is so strong, it actually sub-consciously influences our behavior, both with ourselves and others, our outlook, our self-esteem and even our health. Through these inner words or stickers, we convey and create our emotions, attitudes and feelings, whether we feel happy and excited or discouraged or sad.

Though most people are very conscious about how they communicate with others, they are blissfully unaware of how they communicate or talk to themselves and the colossal damage it can create. But whether we realize it or not, we are constantly thinking or mentally talking to ourselves.

It's estimated, according to the National Science Foundation, that the average person thinks a mind boggling 12-60,000 thoughts a day, 80 % of which are negative and a whopping 95% are repetitive; then we wonder why our lives are so hard to change. Whether you're chatting, listening, texting, watching TV, cooking, shopping, travelling, working or exercising, you're thinking and exactly like children's stickers, your self-talk or thoughts can be either positive or negative, the choice is up to you.

Negative Self-Talk - is limiting, self-depreciating and depressing i.e. -

'I'm fat. Useless. I hate myself.
I'll never get a better job.
I'll always be continually broke and in debt.'

Positive Self-Talk - is uplifting and makes you feel great.

'I'm happy and healthy. I respect and love myself.
I'm incredibly lucky.
I am becoming richer every single day'

Change your thoughts and you literally change your life, by creating a new one. From today become aware and listen to your inner voice, to hear how you are treating yourself. You may be shocked. Though we resent people saying nasty things about us, you'd be surprised how often we say them to ourselves. Realize your words, good or bad, are nothing more than a habit, a decision you reached about yourself maybe eons ago, that you simply never changed.

> *"Whether you think you can, or whether you think you can't, either way, you're right."*
> Henry Ford - Founder of Ford Motor Co.

So often for many folks, it's easier to believe the worse than the best about themselves, even when it's untrue. Unfortunately for some inexplicable reason, many people equate negativity with reality and wrongly assume that being positive is somehow unrealistic, but the fact is, your life mirrors your thoughts. It's as straight forward as that. Simply decide once and for all what you want, and stop those negative, self-limiting thoughts.

If you yearn to be rich, stop affirming your lack of poverty by constantly thinking and telling yourself that you are poor, for if you continually tell yourself that you are broke, you will continue to be so. Your negative statements such as "I am poor" will instruct the inner self to *be* poor and so you in turn will become or remain poor. It's only logical; how can you possibly become rich or enjoy a healthy relationship with money, if you're constantly bombarding it with limiting statements, such as you don't have any? But like any habit, self-talk can be changed, for if you start to believe and tell yourself you are rich, over time, that will indeed, become your reality

> *"The only thing standing between you and your goal is the bullshit story you keep telling yourself, as to why you can't achieve it."*
> Jordan Belfort - Wolf of Wall Street.

It's a fact, even before they were rich, affluent people never entertained poor or negative thoughts or self-talk, instead they constantly saw or imagined themselves as *already* prosperous, for they knew categorically that they were in the process of *becoming* rich, no matter how their financial situation contradicted that. They knew quite simply, that it was impossible to become rich if they constantly undermined or contradicted themselves by thinking or saying poor thoughts. It simply could not happen.

From today, challenge your inner critic and replace all those negative restricting statements with positive, uplifting and courageous ones. A powerful way to do this is through Daily Affirmations.

Affirmations are short, positive statements you make about yourself that you repeat over and over. They are always said or written in the present tense, as though they are actually happening and state exactly what you want rather than what you don't want. They should additionally contain the word, *I, am, me or my*. Affirmations must be personal to you and reflect your goals and ideals. The more you repeat them, the more powerful they become.

Remember, *don't* state what you don't want...

> *"I don't want to be overweight ".*
> *"I think I'll always be in debt."*
> *"I reckon I'm fated to be on my own."*

State what you *do* want...

> *"I am really slim, fit and healthy."*
> *"Money comes easily to me, every single day."*
> *"I am happy, fulfilled and in a loving relationship."*

Write your affirmations down on 3 by 5 cards then place the cards in prominent positions around your home, or somewhere that is personal to you. Practice reading or saying your affirmations in private, a minimum of three times a day, preferably in front of a mirror. If this feels awkward or strange in the beginning, state your affirmations as though you are in the process of becoming what you wish ie..

> *"Every day, I'm becoming more and more confident."*

Whenever you say your statements, believe them to be true. The more enthused you feel, the quicker your affirmations will materialize.

At first, as you state your affirmation, a niggling feeling inside your head will prevail and tell you that you're lying, that what you are saying simply isn't true. Essentially, your beliefs are being tested, for your reality is telling you one thing, while you're trying to pretend something else. This is perfectly normal, but here's where you must make a superhuman jump of faith and believe or choose to believe, in what has not yet materialized. It's vital now to trust in the power of the unseen future, rather than what you see in your current reality. In the words of other successful people, you literally have to "fake it till you make it", believing in your, as yet 'unrevealed' dream, instead of your present situation.

> *"It happened around 5 years ago but it's sort of like a mantra.*
> *You repeat it to yourself every day.*
> *"Music is my life. Music is my life.*
> *The fame is inside of me.*
> *I'm going to make a number one record and*
> *the number one hit." And it's not yet, it's a lie.*
> *You're saying a lie over and over and over again*
> *but then one day, the lie is true."*
> *Lady Gaga - Singer, Songwriter & Actress*

If there is any doubt or negative undercurrent, affirmations simply won't work, for the most important component of all is feeling. Doubts will not only delay or cancel out all your good work, but could effectively stop you from receiving anything and everything you desire, for it's those feelings, not just your words, that will bring about change. Chanting or saying positive words with no underlying passion is a total waste of time, you might as well forget the whole thing. Feelings and beliefs are what move mountains and change both worlds and lives. Though words are truly one of the most powerful things on the planet, the speeches or words that have made history or shaped our world, have always been spoken with both passion and conviction, without them, they would have fallen on deaf ears and been lost in the midst of time.

Ensure all your wonderful words materialize by making affirmations a part of your daily routine. Have faith they will happen, then stand back and watch, as you literally *speak* your words into reality.

FAMOUS LAST WORDS

For Your Child

*"Labels are for filing. Labels are for clothing.
Labels are not for people."*
Martina Navratilova - Tennis Player & Coach

*"Speak to your children as if they are the wisest,
kindest, most beautiful and magical humans on earth,
for what they believe, is what they'll become."*
Brooke Hampton – Writer, Business Owner

*"Children are not things to be molded,
but are people to be unfolded."*
Jess Lair – Author

*"The way we talk to our children,
becomes their inner voice."*
Peggy O'Mara - Author

For You

*"If you want your life to be more rewarding
you have to change the way you think."*
Oprah Winfrey - Media Executive, TV Host

*"The inner speak, your thoughts,
can cause you to be rich or poor,
loved or unloved, happy or unhappy,
attractive or unattractive, powerful or weak."*
Ralph Charell – Author

*"Talk to yourself
like you would to someone you love."*
Brene Brown

*"Everything you attract into your life
is a reflection of the story you believe
and keep telling yourself."*
Farshad Asl - Author & Coach

*"Your whole life is a manifestation of the thoughts,
that go on in your head."*
Lisa Nichols - Motivational Speaker

*"If you hear a voice within you say you cannot paint,
then by all means paint,
and that voice will be silenced."*
"Vincent Van Gogh - Post-Impressionist Painter

Chapter 3 – SKIPPING ROPES

Part 1 - For Your Child

ROUTINES

*"Routines have a very humanizing effect.
Everything gets reduced to essentials."*
Meryl Streep – Film & Stage Actress

When children excitedly jump up and down, chanting a popular song or rhyme, there is a rhythm to their skipping, a rhythm they can depend on. The rope doesn't suddenly jerk all over the place on its own accord at differing heights or tensions, for they'd be unable to skip. Instead it is grasped firmly in your child's hand, so he or she has total control over it. When someone else holds the rope for them, the child trusts that the person won't try to trip them up or hurt them. They in turn keep to their regular rhythm to avoid just that.

It's hard sometimes in this hectic fast paced world to maintain a pattern or rhythm to your life especially if you are a single parent and constantly multi-tasking. But routines are essential for both yourself and your child, for they provide security, a framework and something on which your child can depend, especially toddlers. Kids actually thrive on structures, especially if they are consistent and easy to understand. Structures help avoid unnecessary upset and aggravation, not only for you but for the whole family.

Unfortunately, many of us tend to rush through life forgetting how good it actually feels to slow down and hang out together as a family. People return home after work or school, gobble dinner, do chores then either text, Facebook or veg out in front of the TV or IPad, some families barely even acknowledging or communicating with each other. Others hope they can escape the rat race by moving abroad, in order to rediscover and experience a more wholesome, freer way of life, sipping a glass of vino rosso in Italy, Spain or France. Though I can highly recommend living overseas as a fantastic experience, having lived happily in six countries myself, I believe a contented and wonderful life can be attained anywhere, it's simply a matter of choice. Instead of running yourself to the ground, sit down and plan out a routine.

Three Simple Suggestions

1. Organize Regular Meal times
Start by enjoying a healthy breakfast together, it really takes no time at all to prepare, even if it is just a bowl of cereal, some fruit, yogurt or toast. Wake your children at least one hour before it is time to leave for school, so they have adequate time, it truly is a much nicer and healthier way to start the day, rather than simply scooting out the door. In the evening, eat dinner together as a family around the table so your kids get the opportunity to talk and share their day with you and vice versa. If you're planning a late night or a dinner out, notify your child ahead of time. If they're very young, allow them to have a longer or extra nap in the afternoon or in the car.

2. Instigate a Homework Schedule

Establish a regular homework time to help your child complete their work, maybe a half hour or so before or after dinner. If homework is done in the living room, switch off the T.V. or other distractions and provide your child with some quiet time. Alternatively, find a suitable desk or table close by, away from the noise, so your child isn't ostracized to their room. It's far more civilized and gratifying for them and you, to do their work in company, giving you a quiet moment to catch up with your reading, paperwork or other chores.

3. Employ a Bedtime Routine

"Anyone who thinks the art of conversation is dead ought to tell a child to go to bed."
Robert Gallagher - Photographer

From the time your child is an infant, establish consistent nap and bedtime routines. At a set hour, give them a half-hour' notice that bedtime is approaching. Employ a nightly ritual for your child i.e. bathe, clean teeth, change into pajamas, then settle them in bed with a bedtime story or a chat, whichever they prefer. Our wonderful son always preferred to tell *us* a story, which was great! Tuck them in with a teddy or doll, kiss and hug them goodnight then leave them to enjoy a lovely sleep.

Though routines are important, always leave room for flexibility, for parenting isn't just about hard work and timetables it's also about having fun, building great memories and being spontaneous, for no other reason than because you want to.

"As a source of entertainment, conviviality and good fun, she ranks somewhere between a sprig of parsley and a single ice skate."
Dorothy Parker - Poet, Writer Critic & Satirist

Take a look at your life from your child's point of view. Do you have fun together? If you were a kid, would *you* relish spending time with *you*? Are you bubbly and excited about life or dull and detached? People who are bored with life are generally boring themselves. Why not bring out the child in you, go on the swings, be silly with your kids, jump in puddles, or paint and dress up, for there's nothing like a child to keep you young. You'll probably end up having as much fun as your kids, for nobody ever regretted the good times they had, quite the reverse.

Why Not?
Grab a kid's movie together at the local cinema on a Saturday morning, most of which offer fantastic discounted tickets.
Experiment with skating, horse riding, biking, visiting a museum or attending the theatre; bake chocolate brownies, swim, enjoy a bike ride, feed the ducks or savor a picnic in the park or the grounds of a sumptuous stately home.
Go wild, let your kids pick the music at home, then sing or dance like crazy with them. Lay out a variety of crayons, paints, leaves, feathers, coloured jewels and glue, and create a fabulous collage. Loosen up, make a mess but teach your child how to help you clean up after, even if it's just a token tidy up. If they get more covered in paint than the picture, so what? Whenever possible, encompass tidying up as part of the game, not just a chore. Meet your children after school with a tiny gift, or arrange a surprise trip at the weekend.
Allow their friends to sleep over, or treat them to an elegant high tea complete with, scones, delicious clotted cream and jam. Kids will remember and cherish both these moments and you forever, for a lovely surprise can never be over rated!

"There are many ways to measure success, not the least of which is the way your child describes you when talking to a friend."
Unknown.

Part 2 - FOR YOU

CHANGE

"Don't fear change, embrace it."
Anthony J. D'Angelo - Educational Entrepreneur

Maybe you'd like a few surprises or changes of your own, especially if you feel bored, as though you're trapped by someone else's rules. In the long run a change of routine could make both you and your family a lot happier, for the saddest two words in the English language really are "if only". The things you most regret in life, are usually the risks you didn't take.

Charting Your Own Course
If there's something out of the ordinary you want to do and it isn't detrimental to yourself and your family, then go for it. Follow that burning desire and improve your life. Don't be a passenger on the sea of life, passively bobbing along for the ride, with no idea of your destination. Take charge. Become your own captain and charter your own course. Be brave, for change frequently entails taking a risk and stepping out into the unknown. But diversions can be an exciting and wonderful breath

of fresh air, for as one window of opportunity shuts, another invariably opens.

> *"Why do people wait to hit rock bottom before they are motivated enough to act? It's the heart afraid of breaking that never learns to dance."*
> *Bette Midler – Singer, Actress & Comedienne*

For some folks, moving beyond one's comfort zone can feel uncomfortable. People like to commiserate together or complain endlessly about their jobs, relationships and or other situations and then do absolutely zip about it. Others never complain but secretly feel stuck. Many believe the saying "better the devil you know than the devil you don't know". But why is it better? Often that is simply not true. Perhaps, once upon a time, for example, being miserable in your job, was almost the norm, a trade off you endured if you wanted a steady pay cheque. But nowadays that is not the case, for we are surrounded by endless opportunities such as further education, running a business from home, working part time or training for a career. Options are available for literally anyone willing to take the plunge, including you.

If you believe in your heart, it's time for a change, then do it and don't look back. Focus only on the future and the impact that change will bring, for fears are simply counter-productive and will ultimately limit your ability to reach out and discover that new and rewarding experience.

Maybe you are experiencing problems within a marriage or relationship. What if neither party feels listened to nor understood, and you end up arguing about the same stupid things over and over, the problem seemingly escalating, with nothing ever being resolved, leaving both parties feeling sad, disappointed, angry or frustrated? Feeling in fact, that maybe it's time for a change.

Often couples drearily go through the motions of their day, almost on autopilot, with no excitement, joy de vivre, or appreciation of each other and barely any love. What once attracted is either forgotten or is now an aggravation or annoyance. You find in fact, you're no longer best friends, soul mates or even lovers. Suddenly, it's easier to get mad, than reveal your true feelings of disappointment and loneliness. Most times, it seems it's the other person's fault...but is it? Chances are, what you initially fell in love with is still there, thus before instigating that change, it's worth investing both the time and effort, to rediscover and rectify the relationship. Anything can be fixed if both parties want it.

One of the biggest and most destructive factors in relationships, is that couples simply don't spend enough time together, either through choice or work, resulting in them drifting slowly apart. You only have to peruse celebrity magazines to see that this is one of the main reasons why so many famous marriages fail. Statistics indicate that around 42 % of UK marriages, end in divorce.

Sometimes couples seem pretty defeatist, throwing in the towel at the first sign of discord, but if there has been a happy and rewarding partnership in which neither party was betrayed, or nothing cruel, abusive or untoward has occurred, then it's definitely worth fixing and fighting for, before terminating the relationship.

Often, simple communication is the best place to start. Being frank and writing a long honest letter, allows each person to pour their heart out without fear of interruption. Declaring what has gone wrong in the past and suggesting behaviors which would be helpful in the future, creates hope and strengthens bonds. Indeed, expressing the desire to stay together often comes as a welcome surprise to both parties. If the love is still there, it is never too late.

> *"The more you invest in a marriage,*
> *the more valuable it becomes."*
> *Amy Grant – Singer/ Songwriter & Media Personality*

When both partners commit 110% to staying together, they are already on their way to re-establishing a loving and harmonious relationship, and re-kindling their passionate and precious love. A change, for all concerned, that is most hopefully, for the better.

FAMOUS LAST WORDS

For Your Child

"You will always be your child's favorite toy."
Vicki Lansky - Author & Publisher

*"Always kiss your children goodnight,
even if they're already asleep."*
H Jackson Brown - Author

For You

"The measure of intelligence is the ability to change."
Albert Einstein - Theoretical Physicist

*"You are not your mistakes.
They are what you did, not who you are".*
Lisa Lieberman-Wang - Author/ NLP Practitioner

*"I've learned it's important not to limit yourself.
You can do whatever you really love to do,
no matter what it is."*
Ryan Gosling - Actor & Musician

*"Your regrets aren't what you did but what you didn't do,
so I take every opportunity."*
Cameron Diaz - Actress & Producer

*"If you don't like the road you're walking,
start paving another one."*
Dolly Parton - Singer, Songwriter, Entrepreneur

*"We all have big changes in our lives
that are more or less a second chance."*
Harrison Ford - Movie Actor

Chapter 4 - BOOKS

Part 1 - For Your Child

READING

*"Our greatest natural resource is
the minds of our children."*
Walt Disney - Founder of Disney Co.

*"When I was a child I devoured every book
I could get my hands on.
I loved losing myself in colourful
and dramatic stories."*
David Walliams - Actor, Writer & TV Personality

What an incredibly sad world it would be without books, for through books we can garner literally everything, on any subject under the sun, from art and architecture, to history, music, humour, literature, and science, all of them enriching our lives. Learning through pictures and reading story books, opens up a whole new world to a young reader, for stories fervently capture their imagination and introduce them to a lifetime of pleasure and achievement.

> *"Don't limit a child to your own learning,*
> *for he was born in another time."*
> Rabbinical Saying

One of the most relaxing and rewarding experiences in life, is to curl up with your child and a great book. Every kid deserves to read and read well, for, given the chance, children will devour books. Help stimulate that hunger, for even a tiny toddler can have fun. Simply scatter around a few fabulous books containing bright, colourful pictures, then read and look at them together.

Ensure your child is comfortable with books, and that they are a part of their everyday life. There is no excuse for childhood illiteracy, especially as our libraries are free and overflowing with wonderful volumes. Many libraries hold a story-time session once a week when an animated librarian reads a fantastic selection of stories to a group of young children accompanied by their mothers. The kids really do have a blast as incidentally, do the parents.

> *"If you want your children to be intelligent,*
> *read them fairy tales.*
> *If you want them to be more intelligent,*
> *read them more fairy tales."*
> Albert Einstein - Theoretical Physicist

Read stories to your own child over and over, as children revel in familiar tales and will hang on to your words with as much excitement, as if it were the first time they'd heard them. Let your children in turn read to you or, occasionally tell *you* a story. Don't leave teaching solely to school, for a teacher, no matter how talented and inspiring, is still only one person and with thirty or more children of differing abilities, he or she can only do so much. Parents can contribute enormously at home by building on their child's curiosity and what they have already learned at school.

Next time, instead of sticking your kids in front of the TV to keep them occupied, surround them instead with interesting books. Be a great role model and read yourself. Make learning a delight, for education, or the lack of it, will dramatically change your child's life.

"A quality education has the power to transform societies in a single generation, provide children with the protection they need from the hazards of poverty, labor exploitation and disease, and give them the knowledge, skills and confidence to reach their full potential."
Audrey Hepburn - Film & Stage Actress UNICEF Goodwill Ambassador

Part 2 – FOR YOU

EDUCATION

*"Everyone probably thinks that I'm a
raving nymphomaniac, that I have
an insatiable sexual appetite, when
the truth is I'd rather read a book."*
Madonna Singer/Songwriter Record Producer & Actress

Shocking though it may seem in this day and age, according to the World Literacy Foundation, one in five of the UK population are so poor at reading they struggle to read a medicine label or use a cheque book. Although less than 1% of adults in England would be described as "completely illiterate," a whopping 16% or 5.2 million adults in England, could be described as "functionally illiterate". In other words, they would not pass an English GCSE and have literacy levels at or below those expected of an eleven-year-old. There's absolutely no excuse for this seriously appalling situation, when so much help and education is at hand and so readily available.

As a child enjoys learning, so should we. Besides keeping you smart and the brain and memory active and alert, learning also fights off disabling diseases such as dementia. Many folks should take a leaf out of Judy Dench's book, as the intrepid actress apparently memorizes a new poem or word every day, to help keep her memory intact.

> *"I love being a mother. I think it's the best thing I've ever done, and I personally feel that it's had a very positive effect on my work. I think it's an encouraging force for creativity, it feeds creativity – it did for me certainly."*
> Kate Bush - Singer, Songwriter & Record Producer

Unfortunately, for many adults, learning stops the day they leave school or college. Life becomes so busy juggling jobs and raising families, that education goes out the window, even perusing a book becomes a rare treat.

> *"Magazines all too frequently lead to books and should be regarded as the heavy petting of literature"*
> Fran Lebowitz - Author & Public Speaker

To some families, a gossip magazine or an Argos catalogue is about the closest they ever get to reading. Though these are all well and good, they are utterly inadequate when a plethora of great books are out there, on every single topic imaginable. To live in this world and starve yourself from such a wonderful feast of literature, is truly a tragic mistake.

> *"There is more to us than we know. If we can be made to see it, perhaps for the rest of our lives we will be unwilling, to settle for less."*
> Kurt Hahn - Educator

So often women seem to think they are compelled to choose between work or staying home and looking after their children, believing that by giving up work, they are also giving up anything and everything academic or intellectual. But the reverse is true, for a whole new stimulating world can open up and be yours for the taking. There are so many things you can learn from home, such as studying a new language, courtesy of your local library. Maybe you've always wanted to get a degree, study law, accountancy, architecture, fashion, literature, engineering, online trading, web developing or catering; perhaps you'd like to improve your computer skills, become an artist, learn interior design or music, or simply expand your vocabulary by learning a different word a day.

If you are enthralled with the cut and thrust of politics and wish to understand our political system better but are unsure where to begin, an excellent place is www.parliament.uk or grab a copy of the fascinating book "British Politics for Dummies".

> *"It was through Scholarships, financial*
> *aid programs and work-study*
> *where my earnings from a job on*
> *campus went directly towards my tuition –*
> *that I was able to attend University.*
> *And without question, it was worth every effort."*
> Meghan Markle - Duchess of Sussex

To master a new skill, simply contact your local college or university and ask them to send you a prospectus, for all the full and part time courses available. Many colleges run their own clubs and societies that you can join as a student. Membership is usually only a few pounds and gives you access to a wide variety of clubs. In addition, local papers, magazines and notice boards scattered around town, regularly advertise a variety of inspiring opportunities from dance lessons and amateur dramatics to playing the keyboard or jewelry making. Sports and leisure centres also offer an abundance of classes including aqua aerobics, yoga and trampolining.

For home study, try the Open University at www.open.ac.uk
To improve your English and Maths click on to www.bbc.co.uk/skillswise a great site which aims to help adults improve their reading, writing and number skills.

Maybe deep inside, you fancy trying something different, setting a short time aside either daily or weekly when you can hone a new skill or change your career. Many women bolster their income by hosting cosmetic or fashion parties. You might even have a unique idea for a business that you'd like to instigate from home, but don't know where to start. To receive practical advice or information about starting a new business, why not attend a part-time business course at your local college or for a wealth of information about kick-starting a business check out the following;
www. gov.uk/business-support-helpline
www.gov.uk/browse/business

"I knew that if I failed I wouldn't regret that,
but I knew the one thing I might regret, is not trying."
Jeff Bezos - Amazon Founder & CEO

    Many of our high street banks offer free start-up guides and/or give access to local professionals who can offer qualified, tailored advice to suit your business. Indeed, some of the UK's brightest entrepreneurs grew their businesses from home, because of the huge and obvious advantages including, no office rent or commute to work, flexible hours and trusted and enthused employees!
    Working from home has huge potential, even if you start your business from the humble kitchen table, a bedroom or a converted shed. Indeed, the hugely successful Laura Ashley started her empire, alongside her husband Bernard, from their kitchen table in their London flat, designing placemats, scarves, tablecloths, aprons and even dresses. According to Home Business Opportunities there are now around 2.9 million home businesses in the UK with approximately 1400 new businesses initiated every week, contributing to a colossal £300 billion in annual turnover to the UK economy, many of these businesses started by mums, young people and the over 50's.

"If you think you're too small to have an impact, try going to bed with a mosquito."
Anita Roddick - Founder of the Body Shop

Don't be rigid, use this wonderful time at home with kids to improve and expand your talents, for everything you wish to learn is literally a click away. Learning additional skills will not only improve your job or career prospects but could enhance your entire financial future.

When it comes to learning, it is never too late. In five years you could be 30, 35 or 50, with or without that new skill or talent, so wouldn't it be better to have it? If there is something that you want to learn, learn it and learn it now. If you have a passion for something, you usually do it well and if you do it well, you are normally rewarded both financially and every other way. That burning idea or talent might just be the key to your happiness and future success, so come on what are you waiting for? Put on your thinking cap and dive in!

FAMOUS LAST WORDS

For Your Child

*"Make it a rule never to give a child a book
you would not read yourself."
George Bernard Shaw - Playwright*

*"The important thing is not so much
that every child should be taught,
as that every child should be given the wish to learn."
John Lubbock - Statesman*

*"Upon our children, how they are taught,
rest the fate or fortune of tomorrow's world."
B.C. Forbes - Author & Founder of Forbes Magazine*

*One child, one teacher, one pen and one book
can change the world.
Malala Yousafzai - Activist, Nobel Prize Winner*

For You

*"Learn everything you can,
anytime you can
from anyone you can.
There will always come a time
when you will be grateful you did."
Sarah Caldwell - Impresario & Opera
Company Director*

*"The minute you're not learning;
I believe you're dead."
Jack Nicholson - Movie Actor & Filmmaker*

*"Education is the most powerful weapon,
which you can use, to change the world."
Nelson Mandela - Political Leader & South African
President*

*"A person who won't read,
has no advantage over one who can't read."
Mark Twain – Writer, Publicist & Lecturer*

Chapter 5 - BUBBLES, BALLOONS AND KITES

Part 1 – For Your Child

SHOOTING FOR THE MOON

"Our most important task as a nation, is to make sure all our young people, can achieve their dreams."
Barack Obama - 44th President of the Unites States

Beautiful and rainbow-like, little children gaze in wonder, as bubbles seem to take on a life of their own and drift ever upwards into the azure sky. Bursting with excitement, your child chases after them, bright eyed and rosy cheeked as he tries to catch them. Kids squeal with delight their faces flushed, as they run clutching a balloon or marvel at a kite flying high in the clouds, all of them, in their own way, like your child's dreams and imagination, endless and wonderful.

"There are only two lasting bequests we can hope to give our children. one is roots; the other, wings."
Hodding Carter - U.S. Diplomat

Never burst your child's balloon or tell them that their dreams are full of hot air or that they won't amount to anything. Dreams are magical to young kids and so they should be. Even if their aspirations seem nonsensical or pie in the sky, it's fine, for as your child grows up, so too will their dreams. If they want to fantasize about living in a golden palace, sprinkled with diamonds, let them. Fire their imagination, encourage them to dream and dream big, the bigger the better, with no limit, exactly like the sky. What's the point of dreaming small?

Let them know that in life they really can *do, be* or *have* everything they want, as can *you*. Who are we to say they can't? Let them adopt the incredibly positive and exciting American attitude of 'I can' rather than the frequently more tentative British attitude 'can I'? Children are fueled with endless possibilities and there is nothing wrong with their desires, no matter how fantastic they may seem, for every success started in life as a dream. Don't stifle or destroy them before your child's life has even begun. As your child clutches the strings of their balloons, take his or her hand in yours. One day your child will let go of those strings, as you too will let go of their hand, but the heartstrings between you will never be broken. Because of your love and support, their dreams will soar and evolve into attainable goals; goals that with their continued belief, will someday turn into the incredible reality of their life.

Part 2 - FOR YOU

WISHES, DREAMS AND GOALS

*"It's not only children who grow. Parents do too.
As much as we watch to see what our children
do with their lives, they are watching us
to see what we do with ours.
I can't tell my children to reach for the sun.
All I can do is reach for it myself."*
Joyce Maynard - Writer

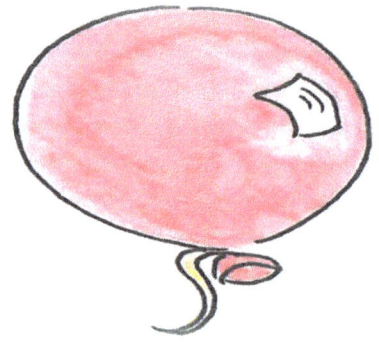

*"We are all in the gutter but some of us,
are looking at the stars."*
Oscar Wilde - Author Playwright & Poet

So what about your own wishes, dreams and goals? In your heart, do you secretly harbour a burning desire to break free, change or improve your life, win millions on the lottery and never have to experience stress or money problems again? Do you watch Ex–Factor, study the financial times, drool over properties in Country Life, or read Hello magazine and fantasize about living in a mansion, jetting across the world, staying in palatial hotels and dressing in designer clothes? Maybe you long to fall in love, to find that special person or soul mate and enjoy romantic rendezvous whilst being serenaded at dusk on a gondola in Venice?

Perhaps you've suffered stressful or painful health problems and you simply wish for peace or better health, either for yourself or your loved ones. You may want to shed those extra pounds and be slim and healthy or begin an exciting new career. Deep inside, do you yearn for things you believe you may never have?

Through your eyes, maybe it seems like this is *it* for you, this is your lot, your life, all you will ever aspire to or achieve. Possibly you feel that whilst others live a seemingly charmed existence, yours is full of struggle and strife and that this is as good as it gets. Maybe there are so many things in life that you'd like to change, you just don't know where to start. But the answer is simple. You start with *you*. It's so much easier to change your deep rooted beliefs, than try the impossible task of changing the world around you. Very often, whether we realize it or not, the greatest obstacle of all to achieving a better life, is often our own self-doubt.

To remove that doubt, you must first realize the **difference** between a **Wish**, a **Dream** and a **Goal**.

A Wish - is something you might desperately desire but actually have no intention of taking any action to get; it's wishful thinking, pie in the sky, which is all well and good, but unless it's converted into a dream and a goal, chances are that's all it will ever remain.

A Dream - is completely different. Dreams can be huge, seemingly unrealistic, even implausible, at first glance but a dream represents something you really want; something that is utterly attainable. A dream is something you're prepared to work at or struggle for, an ideal or target, you are passionate about, a destination or lifestyle you wholeheartedly desire for yourself, either short or long term.

> *"I remember my mum once said "I suppose you'll give it a year and see if you can make it as an actress? And I said "No mum, I think I'll give it ten."*
> Olivia Colman - Film & TV Actress

A Goal - Goals are the vital steps or actions you must take, along the way, to achieve that dream. Like signposts on a roadmap, they take you from where you are, to where you want to be.

If a dream is your destination, then goals keep you focused on your road to success. Goals give you something to aim for, a single objective to harness your time and energy on, even for a few hours at a time. Though goals are inspired by your dreams, they are a lot more detailed. Unfortunately, the majority of us never bother with goals, let alone dreams, often because people don't have a clue what they truly want. Maybe they are too busy or disorganized, frightened of failure, rejection or the unknown. Whatever the reason, they neglect to set or recognize the value of goals as a means to their success. Other times people are simply so overwhelmed by all the changes they wish to make; they end up abandoning everything before they've even begun. But, goal setting is like a muscle, the more you use it the stronger it becomes. Goals help you remember the reasons why, help you recall the big picture, the dreams you have and your ultimate destination.

> *"I never said: "Well I don't have this and I don't have that".*
> *"I said: "I don't have this but I'm going to get it"."*
> Tina Turner - Singer/Songwriter Dancer & Actress

In order to stay motivated and persistent, you have to ask yourself first and foremost, "What is your dream?" What do you really want out of life? What is the reason you are prepared to put time, effort, maybe even money into your desires? When the reasons *why* are important enough, just watch as the world changes, to accommodate you.

> *"People with goals succeed because they know where they are going. It's as simple as that."*
> Earl Nightingale - Founder of Nightingale Conant Corporation

Allocate some quiet time and sit down and decide exactly what you want out of life; be it love, more money, a better house, financial freedom, a new career or even a holiday abroad. Think about it. If someone could wave a magic wand and give you whatever you desired, what would it be? What would you like to *have, do* or *be* in life? Perhaps this is the only time you've ever asked yourself that question. Perhaps for the first time in your life you are giving yourself space and permission to discover the real you, the true essence of who you are.

Next, write your dream down, the only criteria being that it has to be believable to you. Be bold, brave and fearless but above all, be totally honest, for the world really is yours for the taking.

Write your dream in the present tense, never in the future, for chances are, if you do, that's precisely where it will remain and thus will probably never happen. Determine what you *want* for your future, not what you don't want. Yet again, don't write what you *don't* want ie

> *"I don't want to struggle and be poor anymore."*
> *I don't want to stay overweight and unhealthy"*
> *"I don't want to continue in this awful job."*

Write what you *do* want.

> *"I want to be rich and have a constant flow of money."*
> *"I want to be slim and healthy and look and feel great".*
> *"I want a wonderful and rewarding new career."*
> *"I want someone special in my life"*

Describe your dream in detail. If it's a new house you desire, don't simply jot down –

> *"I want a new house."*

Instead, describe precisely what you desire....

> *"In the shortest time possible I want a modern detached
> 3 bed, 3 bath home in a quiet, leafy cul-de-sac
> in (whatever area), with a large garden,
> close to all the local schools, shops and other amenities,
> for around £400,000."*

The more information you supply the better it is.

If you wish for money, decide exactly how much money you want, what you'd like to do with it and the lifestyle you would love to live, then picture yourself being rich. If you wish to lose weight, how many kilos or pounds do you want to lose and by what time? Be specific about your desires, this is no time to be vague, for just the writing of goals can set the whole process in motion. Jotting down or asking for your dreams, is a huge first step towards actually achieving them.

Anticipate your dream with confidence and excitement then get on with your life, knowing undoubtedly that it will appear or materialize in your life. When you book a holiday or order an item on Amazon, you only do it once, not over and over again. You don't keep placing the same order, as you're confident it will soon be dispatched and winging its way towards you. Trust from the moment you asked for your dream, it instantly became yours.

Additionally, don't attempt to figure out *how* to make your dream happen, that's not your job or concern and it limits your possibilities and imagination, for you really have no idea of the spectacular opportunities that are waiting for you, around the corner. Realize that you don't have to know at the outset how you are going to achieve your desires, you just have to believe you can do it. Sure, if you have a plan, it makes it easier but it is not essential to have every individual step mapped out in advance, in fact it's better not to, for when you are willing to do whatever it takes, the right steps will reveal themselves; steps that till this point you never envisioned.

There is also an added ingredient that has been called many things, a guardian angel, inspiration, luck, call it what you will. It's that inexplicable, almost magical element that kicks in and helps you attain what you want, when you determine to do something. It's that amazing coincidence of being in the right place at the right time, that sense of destiny, when you just happen to bump into the very person, either known or unknown that you wanted to meet, that somebody who will turn out to be the love of your life or a person that will help you on your voyage of success. It's like a sprinkling of fairy dust, utterly magically, totally random, endlessly unfathomable and truly marvelous. Be on the lookout for these golden opportunities for they can often happen where and when you least expect them. Watch as doors open unexpectedly, setting you on the right course, attracting even more people and circumstances necessary to accomplish your dream. Take advantage of them, then move forward with relentless determination. It may seem as though lady luck is smiling on you. In truth, these opportunities probably always existed, you simply failed to notice them.

Four Tips for Following Your Star

1. First, it's imperative that you make your dreams personal to *you*. Don't set goals for yourself that are really someone else's dream *for* you, perhaps someone you are trying to placate or please. Don't allow them to control you, by convincing you to achieve their desires, for if you succeed, the disappointment will be overwhelming, rather like climbing a colossal mountain only to discover that it is the wrong one. Ensure that the goals you choose are truly the ones that you desire.

Be aware, many times friends and family, often with the very best of intentions, may try to discourage or persuade us to ditch our desires, believing them to be unrealistic. Maybe for them they are. Perhaps they can't appreciate the big picture and the efforts you are making or their vision is simply more limited than yours. Possibly they lack your fire, your drive, your courage or your unfailing belief. Maybe they need security, while you are prepared to take the risks.

> *"You have to stay true to yourself and don't be afraid even though people may say what you're doing isn't cool or isn't right. I promise you, you will not regret it, if you stay true to who you are and what you love to do."*
> Emma Stone - Actress

Sometimes, people can attempt to sabotage your dreams because they are jealous or worried you just might succeed, and they would no longer be able to control you, or in some way exert their own desires or restrictions on you. Don't be swayed but stand your ground. Never become waylaid because of others negativity. Have infinite belief in yourself and don't let anyone or anything de-rail you. If you believe in your dream, believe in your success. Don't let anyone, no matter how close, rob you of that.

2. Be aware, even with commitment, the path won't always be easy, disappointments will certainly arise. It's all part of the journey. When there are frustrations or set-backs along the way, which there undoubtedly will be, say to hell with them, stay focused and remain positive, no matter what. You may be tempted to abandon your dream, but if it's still what you desire, *don't*. In the wise words of Sir Winston Churchill. *"Never, never, never give up."* Whatever happens, keep motivated. Know that whatever it takes you are going to get there. You are going to succeed. If you're determined, you'll overcome any setbacks, for nothing in the world will stop you. Stick to it, become a winner, think of the end result and you will surely triumph!

3. Realize that, in order to be successful one must accept that failure or obstacles, are part of one's success. It's very rare for anything to be accomplished on the first attempt. Thomas Edison failed over a thousand times before he finally discovered a way to make the light bulb work. But in his mind, did he see it as failure? Not at all. He'd discovered a thousand ways of how *not* to do it. As he declared…

> *"Many of life's failures are people who did not realize how close they were to success when they gave up."*

Never be frightened to fail, failure is good. It's from failure we learn. Failure will help you garner your success. Obstacles or opportunities as we should rightfully view them, are mere stepping-stones on your stairway to heaven, for the opposite of winning is not failure, it's not even trying. That inactivity will definitely guarantee your failure.

> *"Don't let rejection create self-doubt. The founder of Starbucks was turned down by 217 of the 242 investors, he initially spoke with."*
> Elizabeth Galbut - Venture Capitalist

In truth, every successful entrepreneur, business mogul, writer, sports person, entrepreneur, judge, singer, model, actress, scientist and artist have all failed along the way. The difference was they had the courage of their convictions and refused point blank to quit or give up. As they say "strap on a pair" until you make your dream your reality.

4. Along the way stop and review or re-write your goals, during your fantastic adventure. Make comparisons with where you are, compared to where you were. Are you still heading in the right direction? If not, adjust or fine tune your goals and breathe new life into them. Make both your goals and yourself a force that cannot be stopped. Be excited about your goals and envis-

age your life and dreams. Relish both the incredible journey *and* your final, magnificent destination.

"You have this one life. How do you wanna spend it? Apologizing? Regretting? Questioning? Hating yourself? Dieting? Running after people who don't see you? Be brave. Believe in yourself. Do what feels good. Take risks. You have this one life. Make yourself proud."
Cara Delevingne - Model & Actress

FAMOUS LAST WORDS

For Your Child

"Teach your children they're unique. That way, they won't feel pressured to be like everybody else."
Cindy Cashman - Author & Agent

"You sort of start thinking anything is possible, if you've got enough nerve."
J.K. Rowling - Author Harry Potter & Novelist

"Parents can plant magic in a child's mind through certain words spoken with some thrilling quality of voice, some uplift of the heart and spirit."
Robert MacNeil - Novelist, News Anchor & Journalist

For You

"The greatest glory in living lies not in never falling, but in rising every time we fall."
Nelson Mandela - Activist & President of South Africa

"The only failure is not to try."
George Clooney - Actor, Director & Producer

"Your time is limited, so don't waste it living someone else's life."
Steve Jobs - Co-Founder of Apple

"One's real life is so often the life, that one does not lead."
Oscar Wilde - Poet & Playwright

*"What people say isn't going to stop me.
I have to do things for myself."*
Kate Moss - Super Model

*"Stop thinking in terms of limitations
and start thinking in terms of possibilities."*
Terry Josephson - Motivational Speaker

*"Nothing is impossible, the word itself says
' I'm possible'."*
Audrey Hepburn - Actress & Humanitarian

*"The people who get on in this world are the people
who get up and look for the circumstances they want,
and if they don't find them, make them."*
George Bernard Shaw - Playwright

*"Shoot for the moon. Even if you miss it
you will land among the stars."*
Les Brown - Author & Motivational Speaker

Chapter 6 - KITCHENS AND COOKERS

Part 1 - For Your Child

HEALTHY EATING

*"It's bizarre that the produce manager is
more important to my children's health, than the Pediatrician."*
Meryl Streep – Stage & Film Actress

Kids love nothing more than pottering around a pretend cooker, whipping up a culinary masterpiece, then proudly serving up their offerings; usually the coloured plastic chicken, veg and pineapple that we're all so familiar with. Their shiny peas and fish are presented with all the panache of an expensive gourmet meal. But if the food didn't look so appealing, kids wouldn't have nearly as much fun.

Pretend food and kitchens are great for learning, as they emulate real life products that their parents use on a daily basis. It's important therefore to steer them in the right direction, for good nutritious food is essential. There's no getting around it, kids really are what they eat. Food should make them look and feel terrific and provide them with boundless energy; no short cuts or excuses here. I can't be bothered or "I can't cook" really doesn't cut the mustard, especially when healthy food is so inexpensive, quick and easy to prepare.

> *"Many kids can tell you about drugs but do not know what celery or courgettes taste like……*
> *I challenge you to go to any school and open 50 lunch boxes and I guarantee you there will be one or two cans of red bull, they'll be cold McDonalds and jam sandwiches with several cakes……*
> *Give your kids a bloody knife and fork and let me put some food in front of them they can eat."*
> *Jamie Oliver - Celebrity Chef & Author*

Equally, giving a kid a bag of crisps for breakfast before school is indefensible. How on earth is a child supposed to concentrate and feel energized on that? Having a burger and chips for dinner is fine occasionally but not as a way of life, same with fizzy drinks. I believe deep down, parents know that. Encourage your kids to drink water, milk or diluted squash, knocking those dreadful sugar-laden fizzy drinks firmly on the head.

At meal times, avoid feeding kids food like chicken nuggets, chips or pizza on a regular basis, because you've no inkling how to prepare anything else. Nowadays there are literally thousands of cook books available, starting from the basics of boiling an egg to producing a culinary masterpiece, so there really is no excuse to plead that you can't cook. You can even go on line and type in the dish or meal that you want. In an instant, you'll have an easy to follow recipe that's both inexpensive, delicious and simple to prepare.

Nobody can do anything until they try, it's as simple as that, and cooking is no exception. Often it's a choice of simply not wanting to cook but if kids grow up eating properly they will continue that vital legacy throughout their lives. Something that struck me while living in Italy was how the parents or mother would often come home from work and somehow within minutes, a mouth-watering and delicious feast would appear on the table. As people all around the Mediterranean know, good food and enjoyable company is something to be savoured.

> *"You could probably get through life without knowing how to roast a chicken, but the question is, would you want to?"*
> *Nigella Lawson - Gourmet & TV Personality*

    Introduce healthy eating as a matter of course, cultivating your child's natural tendency towards consuming and enjoying nourishing food. Youngsters can only eat what you dish up, so as parents it's up to us to serve the very best, tastiest meals we can, and that doesn't have to cost a fortune, especially if you buy fruits and vegetables that are in season. Lentils are also extremely satisfying, filling and highly nutritious. Look out for store discounts on certain cuts of meat, cheese or fish besides serving substitutes such as tofu. Limit treats such as, biscuits, cakes, crisps, fatty foods, chocolate, sweets and pastries. Check also that your child doesn't consume too much salt, definitely less than the six grams a day recommended for adults. As bacon, ham and sausages all contain a fair amount, it's best to ration them too.

    If you're too busy or tired in the evening to cook a wholesome meal then treat yourself and your family by investing in a hot-pot or slow cooker, most of which come accompanied with their own easy to follow cook book. Meals take around 15-20 minutes to prepare in the morning and then cook slowly all day. They are incredibly tasty, highly nutritious, inexpensive and a breeze to prepare. At the end of the day, you can come home, sit back and enjoy a delicious home-made meal. If preparing dinner every day seems too much of an effort, remember with the right planning, you need only cook a few times a week and space it out as you go along.

"The early years are when you give your child a foundation for establishing a proper diet. If kids learn about the importance of eating healthy early in their lives, they will not have to relearn as an adult."
Nicole Henderson - Wife & mother of three kids

With obesity and Type two diabetes now on the rise, it really makes sense to eat right especially as the link between diet and behavior has long been established. Fill a kid full of sugar, and how, in all honesty, would you expect him to react? Kids deserve a balanced healthy diet; if they don't get it from home, where will they?

The Fabulous Four
Selecting foods daily from these four main categories, will help ensure your kids receive all the nutrition, vitamins and minerals they need.

1. Bread, Cereals, Potatoes, Couscous, Pasta or Rice - For energy, minerals and vitamins - Make these a main staple of your meal.
2. Fruit & Vegetables - For fibre, vitamins, minerals and iron. Eat a wide variety and aim for at least five portions a day.
3. Milk & Dairy Foods - i.e. Cheese and Yoghurt, for healthy teeth and strong bones. Also great sources of protein, vitamin A and B12.
4. Meat, White & Oily Fish, Poultry, Eggs, Pulses, Beans, Nuts & Seeds - For protein, vitamins, minerals and iron.

If you find your child is reluctant to improve or change some of his or her eating habits, don't worry for there are all sorts of ingenious and appetizing ways, you can get them to eat healthily.

1. Cut out canned or convenience foods and add fresh veggies to favourite dishes i.e. finely sliced mushrooms, carrot, celery, onions and red peppers to Bolognese.
2. Top jacket potatoes with cheese and grated carrot, or mash swede and carrot together with a little butter, then add to mashed potato. Alternatively, roast some delicious sweet potatoes and mash with butter. If your kids crave chips, serve up some home-made potato wedges instead. Cut the potatoes in their skins into wedges, brush with a little olive oil and bake in the oven (170C/325F) until they are soft in the middle and deliciously crisp on the outside.
3. Make a dip and use cut peppers, celery, carrot and cauliflower florets as the sticks.
4. For snacks try a selection of nuts, dried fruit, sesame or sunflower seeds, raisins, slices of banana or orange or satsuma segments.
6. Instead of salt, flavour foods with either fresh or dried herbs, spices, a dash of Balsamic vinegar or lemon juice.

Allow a young child to make his or her own choices ie. whether they prefer broccoli or peas. Ensure portions aren't too big and don't insist on them eating a food they don't like or scraping up every single morsel on their plate. Do this and the meal could very easily end in tears, resulting in your youngster completely turning off that particular food. Introduce exciting new tastes in small servings and offer a wide variety. Make meal times happy and relaxed affairs. As your children grow older, discuss nutrition with them, allowing them to select a few healthy items of their own.

Part 2 - FOR YOU

WEIGHT LOSS

*"If I had been around when Rubens was painting,
I would have been revered as a fabulous model.
Kate Moss? Well, she would have been the paint brush."
Dawn French - English Actress, Writer & Comedienne*

*You look how you look. Be comfortable.
What are you going to do?
Be hungry every single day to make other people happy?
That's just dumb."
Jennifer Lawrence - Actress*

It's a fact, for some reason, most women seem to be perpetually on diets, which in itself shows they generally don't work; how great it would be then to discover a magical elixir that would instantly make us slim? Unfortunately, folks, it doesn't exist. If you do choose to lose weight, there is only one sensible, guaranteed way to do it and there is nothing magical about it, simply eat less and exercise more. Do these two things and the pounds will literally melt away.

The Inside Skinny – Five Tips
To lose weight and stay healthy, try the following.

Tip 1- Think Yourself Slim
It really does work. Visualizing or seeing yourself as already slim provides a powerful mindset that will both help and support you in losing your weight, putting both your sub-conscious and conscious mind in a positive state, from the outset. This in turn will make you less likely to sabotage your diet by setting and meeting realistic weight-loss goals. With this in mind, why not treat yourself to a few items of clothing that are perhaps a size or two smaller than your current size? Look at them often, then plan a special date or occasion in your diary when you can wear them.

> *"People have asked me "Do you starve yourself before photo shoots? 'I always say, "No way. That's what air brushing is for"."*
> *Sarah Michele Gellar - T.V. & Film Actress*

Tip 2 – Eat Only When You Are Hungry
Don't munch mindlessly whist watching TV or reading a book. How many of us stuff our faces with crisps, biscuits or anything edible we can lay our hands on that doesn't take any effort? So often we endlessly scoff to our hearts content, trying to ignore or banish from our conscience the fruitless and pointless calories we are gorging, often on automatic pilot, so we barely even taste or register what or how much we have actually consumed.

Tip 3 – At Dinner Time Utilize Smaller Plates
Serve moderate portions, adhering to the rule of ½ a plate veg ¼ plate protein and a ¼ plate carbohydrate. Eat slower and really appreciate each mouth full, then stop when you are satisfied, not when you feel your stomach is stuffed to the gills and feels like it's about to explode.

*"No one is born a great cook;
one learns by doing so."*
Julia Child - Chef, Author & TV Personality

Instead of frying your food, try to grill, stir fry, bake or casserole it, removing any and all excess fat from the meat before cooking. If you must indulge in a crispy bacon sandwich go ahead, just don't eat one every day. Consume real fruit instead of canned and reduce your sugar intake on drinks and cereals. If like me, you have a weakness for hot chocolate, substitute with a satisfying low calorie option, many of which are equally as good.

Tip 4 – Avoid Snaking Between Meals
Don't graze needlessly through the day out of sheer boredom, fatigue or habit. If you are hungry between meals, wait five minutes then ask yourself from a scale of 1-10 how hungry am I? If it's only 2 or 3, have a drink of water or a small healthy snack i.e. a piece of fruit, a selection of vegetable crudités such as carrots or red peppers, accompanied by a low-fat dip; or a handful of nuts, seeds, dates or raisins, as opposed to crisps, cakes, biscuits, ice cream or chocolate. They may make you feel satisfied for a moment but you'll instantly regret it and chances are, your overwhelming and unforgiving guilt will probably lead you to indulging in ever more calories. Having said that, never prohibit anything as, human nature being what it is, you'll end up craving that forbidden fruit even more. Be sensible and enjoy treats in moderation. If you fancy some chocolate, go for it. Just don't end up shoveling down the whole bar.

Tip 5 – Drink Lots of Water
Drink water regularly throughout the day but also allow yourself an occasional glass of wine with dinner, like the French and Mediterranean peoples, who invariably enjoy healthy diets and lifestyles but passionately enjoy their vino. As the 19th century

French gastronome Jean Anthelme Brillat quite rightly mused *"A meal without wine is like a day without sunshine."*

Besides the obvious delights, it appears red wine has innumerable health benefits as the antioxidants contained in the wine, not only reduces the risk of heart disease but can actually help prevent cancer and assist in lowering cholesterol. After which I think only one word needs to be said,"cheers!"

See this healthy style of eating not as a diet but as a new way of life. If you over eat one day, don't fret, merely balance it out the next. Don't fall into the trap of comfort or emotional eating, justifying that as your excuse. There are always endless cop-outs for you to indulge, including feeling happy or sad, fed up, wishing to celebrate, tired, angry, pleased or bored. Whatever you're feeling, there will *always* be a valid and acceptable reason or excuse to eat drink and be merry. Remember, life is a tradeoff, if you gorge yourself, you *won't* be slim, conversely, if you starve yourself, you'll be miserable, unhealthy and sick.

Strike a happy medium, eat whatever and whenever you like but eat in moderation, that way you really can have your cake and eat it. Make this a lifestyle change, not a diet. Face it, who'd want to live in a permanent state of denial? No one, which is precisely why most diets don't work.

The key to becoming slim in a healthy and enjoyable way is to cut down, not cut out. Don't focus on what you don't want; focus on what you do. No matter how overwhelming your weight loss may seem, never give up but remain determined and stick to your goal. If you're resolute enough, you'll shed those pounds and get there in the end. As you slip on those new clothes, admiring your gorgeous figure, you'll know all your hard work had definitely been worthwhile.

"Thank you for calling the Weight Loss Hotline.
If you'd like to lose a half pound right now
press 1, eighteen thousand times."
Randy Glasbergen - Cartoonist & Humourous
Illustrator

Exercise – Getting a Jump on Your Day

> *"I never mind scrubbing floors, vacuuming or bending or carrying stuff. Each time I do it I think this is instead of going to the gym."*
> Joanna Lumley - English Actress, Model & TV Presenter

Instead of constantly wearing a path from the fridge or biscuit tin to the sofa, start exercising for real. There are so many sports to choose from including the immensely popular High Intensity Interval Training 'HIIT', which involves short bursts of intense exercise and activity, followed by short periods of rest. Most people practice HIIT in a teacher led class, one of the benefits being that you get a great workout in as little as twenty minutes. If that doesn't appeal, why not indulge in a healthy swim, a quick jog, a spot of weight training, Pilates, Yoga or maybe get involved in a team sport? Alternatively, walk. Walking is free, and utterly invigorating, the fresh air promoting a terrific sense of wellbeing, as you enjoy the scenery, be it in a park, a city or by the sea. If you fancy something different, try horse riding, tai chi, rock climbing, belly or tap dancing, hula hooping, or even cheerleading, yet another popular fad from the U.S.

If you find riding a stationary bike, downright boring, listen to music or watch T.V whilst cycling. If working out in public is not your thing, stick in an exercise DVD and exercise at home or play music and simply dance to your heart's content; the benefits both physically, emotionally and spiritually of exercise, are enormous. You'll not only look and feel better, your skin will glow, your hair will be shinier, you'll sleep better and because exercise releases endorphins, you'll feel even happier. Start with 3 x 30 minutes per week of moderate aerobic exercise. If 30 minutes at a time is impossible, break it down to 3 x 10 minute slots. (If you have any doubt about your level of fitness always check with your Doctor before exercising)

Along the way maybe every 7 lb. or 3-4 kilos, reward yourself with a nonfood treat such as a lipstick, a bottle of perfume, an exotic T shirt, hair/sports accessory or a trip to the theatre, anything, just as long as it's not edible. Paste pictures up of something or someone that can inspire you to keep focused and lose the weight. If possible, avoid the temptation to weigh yourself every day as weight continually fluctuates. If you must weigh, do it weekly or preferably on the last day of every month. Better still regularly measure yourself, to see exactly how many inches you've lost. Sometimes, it's easier to see the inches fall off, than the pounds and recording that fantastic inch loss will definitely bolster your resolve, keeping you on track.

It's a fact nobody ever regretted losing excess weight, their only regret was the time it had taken them to make the decision to get started. So come on, what are you waiting for, you've only inches to lose but a world to gain. When the weight is gone, be proud, knowing through sheer will power and determination, you really *did* achieve your goal.

FAMOUS LAST WORDS

For You

*"I've been on a diet for two weeks
and all I've lost is 14 days."*
Totie Fields - Comedienne

*"I'd much rather be known as some curvy
Kate than as some skinny stick."*
Kate Winslet - Actress

*"I'm Jewish. I don't work out.
If God wanted us to bend over,
he'd put diamonds on the floor."*
Joan Rivers - Comedienne, Producer & TV Host

*"You have to stay in shape.
My grandmother, she started walking 5 miles a day
when she was sixty. She's 97 today and
we don't know well the hell she is."*
Ellen DeGeneres – Comedienne & T.V. Host

*"I think everyone has her own body type
and looks good at different weights -
that's what's so beautiful."*
Beyoncé - Singer, Songwriter & Actress

"Dieting is the only game where you win, when you lose."
Karl Lagerfeld - Creative Director, Fashion
Designer & Artist

Chapter 7 - TEA SETS

Part 1 - For Your Child

MANNERS

"One of the greatest questions you have to ask yourself at the end of the day - If I were the only example my child has from whom to learn right from wrong, what would she have learned today?"
Dr Michele Borba - Parenting Expert & Author

With their little pinkies delicately curled and their most endearing manners on display, kids pour tea with so much finesse, one could easily imagine them conducting a graceful Japanese Tea ceremony, their manners are so exquisite. But in the real world, when it comes to eating meals, kids aren't always quite so refined, yet good manners cost nothing to either give or receive; they also provide kids with skills that benefit them for the rest of their lives and ensure they are comfortable, in every part of the world and strata of society.

"Kind students are the coolest."
Heidi McDonald - Writer & Editor

In this day and age, politeness really is appreciated, for good manners are something that will never go unnoticed. If you want your child to stand out from the crowd, teach them manners, for nowadays in some quarters, they are almost a rarity. You'll be delighted at how many compliments you'll both receive.

> *"The test of good manners is to be able to put up pleasantly with bad ones."*
> Wendell Wilkey - Lawyer & Politician

Unfortunately, a lack of manners is by no means restricted to kids. Though most people are generally polite, a small percentage of grown-ups, insist on acting downright aggressive in public, swearing or barging in front of others.

If a child's role model or parent is offensive, ill-mannered or abrupt what chance does that child have? With road rage so prevalent it really is time to stop and analyze, exactly how we are behaving in front of our children. From as young as two or three years onwards a child is able to learn the 'dos' and 'don'ts' of polite conduct. Children learn by example, mostly yours. You can't be rude to kids and then expect them to be polite to others. Manners should be second nature for all of us, for mannered children grow into mannered adults, which in turn makes for a much kinder world.

> *"Children are natural mimics who act like their parents, despite every effort to teach them good manners."*
> Anon

In order to raise polite kids, you must first be a great role model, thus it's imperative to be civil to folks, be it your kids, spouse, neighbour, waitress, shop assistant or whoever, treating everyone with equal respect. Allow your kids to learn a valuable lesson simply by watching you. When your child communicates with you, engage with them. How many times in a coffee shop or supermarket are children blatantly ignored, their words or pleas barely acknowledged, as though they were invisible or so familiar or unimportant, a parent is simply too disinterested or preoccupied with their Smart phone to answer, culminating in the toddler having a full blown tantrum. Subsequently the poor child ends up being unfairly reprimanded by the now embarrassed parent, when it was clearly the parent's fault to begin with, for not properly communicating with the child. Had the parent shown a bit more insight and consideration, the whole situation would probably have been avoided, and that tantrum nipped in the bud. You wouldn't ignore an adult that way, so why on earth would you be so indifferent to the needs of your own child?

Similarly, when you *are* busy or chatting on the phone, give your child a book or some small activity to play with to keep them occupied, for nothing instigates bad behavior more than boredom, a situation that is so easily avoided.

As they grow older, teach children to answer the phone politely and to enquire who is calling. If you are not available, ask them either to take a message or instruct the caller to phone back later. Never let a child disclose their name, address or any information about themselves or inform the caller that they are alone in the house, even if you are expected back any moment. Show your child how to dial 999 in an emergency and always keep your phone number and address written down next to the phone.

> *"Good manners will open doors that the best education cannot."*
> Clarence Thomas - U.S. Supreme Court Justice

As a matter of course, teach your kids to say the magical words 'please' and 'thank you' when they ask for, or receive something, or if someone holds the door for them. It will certainly keep them in good stead for later life. If they've spent time at a friend's home, encourage your children to thank the person for having them over. Recognize that if we expect our kids to say those three illustrious words, we must also voice them too.

> *"All children behave as well as they are treated."*
> Unknown

Council your child to be patient and wait his or her turn, and not talk over or interrupt when someone is speaking. No one can be heard if there are too many voices at once. Tell them gently to wait, then hold their hand or put your arm around them to let them know you appreciate their good behavior and are aware that it is their turn next. If they do override a younger sibling, ask them to wait a moment until the other child has finished. Compliment your child, tell them that you're proud of his or her polite behavior and re-enforce his good actions. If he does something wrong don't be scathing, simply tell him how to do it better the next time and the reason why.

> *"- Pass the salt.*
> *- And what's the magic word?*
> *- Now!"*
> The Addams Family

Good table manners are equally essential, as they're not merely concerned with proper eating but are about being considerate to others. As always your kids will copy *your* behavior so ensure your own manners are impeccable. They don't have to be quite as formal as dining with the Queen, but routinely practice basic etiquette, such as teaching kids not to reach over someone's plate in order to retrieve something but to request instead for the item to be passed. Show your child how to hold their fork properly and to not shovel their food in; it looks gross and a child could easily choke. Children should chew with mouths closed and avoid talking when mouths are full; let kids practice at home by eating meals together at the table, so good manners become a way of life, rather than an exception.

When going to a restaurant, take something along to occupy your child whilst waiting for their meal i.e. paper and crayons, a comic, or maybe just chat.

> *"A person who is nice to you but rude to the waiter, is not a nice person."*
> Dave Berry - Author & Columnist

If the food is not up to scratch, don't make loud or insulting comments to the waiter. Simply register your complaint to the manager or appropriate person. If a piece of silverware falls on the floor, signal the waiter for another.

Reaping What They Sow

> *"My parents taught me about the importance of qualities like kindness, respect and honesty.*
> *I realise how central values like these have been to me throughout my life...*
> *That is why William and I want to teach our little children*
> *...just how important these things are as they grow up.*
> *In my view it's just as important as excelling at math's or sport."*
> Catherine - Duchess of Cambridge

Besides manners, it's enormously important for kids to be kind, for they will soon discover that what they give out they'll get back. Be honest with them about what type of behavior you expect. If your child does something thoughtless or cruel, let them know immediately that their conduct was unacceptable and why it was so. Focus on what the child has done, rather than on the child i.e. (what you *did* wasn't very nice rather than *you* are not very nice) such a huge and important difference.

Teach kids to share their toys and encourage empathy. i.e. if a friend of theirs scrapes their knee or hurts themselves, show your child how to comfort them. As always the thing that will inspire their kindness the most, is the way he or she is treated by *you*. What we teach our kids when they are young, will often determine the actions they will take, when they are adults.

Part 2 – FOR YOU

KINDNESS

"I wanted people not to care about whether you were gay, straight, black, white, transgender, whatever it may be... That being said, there's more work to be done... I still want to change the world, absolutely."
Boy George - Singer Songwriter & DJ

"When you start to develop your powers of empathy and imagination, the whole world opens up to you."
Susan Sarandon - Actress Social & Political Activist

As kindness can empower and uplift a neighbourhood, a lack of it can just as quickly demoralize whole communities. With intolerance, prejudice, foul language and violence so prevalent in some countries, it seems society has become increasingly angrier and more mean spirited than ever, individuals more selfish and blinkered. Isn't it time then, to get a grip?

Kindness is essential in the world, for it connects us with others, makes us human and inspires hope. Kindness should be a basic way of life and practiced 365 days a year, for to be kind brings out the best in humanity. Thankfully, most folks are incredibly compassionate, as evidenced by the generous contributions to charities and by the many heroic acts of selflessness, performed by a whole raft of society who really epitomize what it means to be human and humane.

> *"Kindness is the only service that will stand the storm of life and not wash out."*
> Abraham Lincoln - Statesman & U.S. President

Take a minute and consider, when did you last commit a random act of kindness? The chances are that whatever you did, made you feel just as wonderful in *your* heart as it did for the other person.

   Be considerate to yourself and your family, for like charity, thoughtfulness begins at home. There are a multitude of ways one can demonstrate compassion such as ensuring your kids always feel comfortable and safe, for often it's the little things that count. If a baby cries don't only look to the practical solution i.e. if they're tired, wet or hungry, when sometimes a simple reassuring hug is all that's required.

   When children are very tiny and tucked up in a pushchair, face them towards you, so they can feel secure. As they get older, you can easily reverse the chair the other way. Be vigilant, hold your toddler's hand and never allow them to run ahead of you, down a dangerously busy street. When you go into a warm coffee shop and remove your coat, ensure your child is equally cool and comfortable.

   Most importantly, allow your kids to relax. Don't push them into too many activities or schedule their every moment. Occasionally, kids are paraded around almost like little trophies or an extension of the parent's desires, plugged into so many different interests, they end up stressed and exhausted for no good reason.

Kids need time to unwind and do nothing. Time simply, to be kids.

> *"You are worried about seeing him spend his early years in doing nothing. What! Is it nothing to be happy? Nothing to skip, play and run around all day long? Never in his life will he be so busy again."*
> *Jean – Jacques Rousseau - Philosopher, Writer & Composer*

 Whenever possible, help someone who is in need, be it a neighbour, elderly person, friend or relative. Don't be negative, cynical or deceitful and refrain from idle gossip or spreading vicious rumours. How would you like it done to you? Never stare or make fun of others, no matter how different they may appear. Avoid being judgmental or putting people down, who knows, one day you may also be in their position; it's hard to be objective, if you've never experienced that person's situation or predicament. Most times, people are generally doing the very best they can, who are we to judge if that's sufficient or not?

 It costs nothing to smile, be pleasant and brighten someone's day. Like the sun, your kindness could melt even the loneliest of hearts.

FAMOUS LAST WORDS

For Your Child

"I think probably kindness is my number one attribute in a human being. I'll put it before any of the things like courage or bravery or generosity or anything else."
Roald Dahl - Novelist & Poet

"Live so that when children think of fairness, and integrity, they think of you."
H Jackson Brown - Author Inspirational Books

"Be kind, don't judge and have respect for others. If we can do all this, the world would be a better place. The point is to teach this to the next generation."
Jasmine Guinness - Designer & Model

For You

"Carry out a random act of kindness, with no expectation of reward, Safe in the knowledge that one day, someone might do the same for you."
Princess Diana

"I've never known any human being, high or humble, whoever regretted, when nearing life's end, having done kindly deeds."
B.C. Forbes - Financial Journalist, Founder Forbes Magazine

"I have witnessed the softening of the hardest hearts by a simple smile."
Goldie Hawn - Actress Director & Producer

*"No matter what happens in life, be good to people.
Being good to people is a wonderful legacy
to leave behind."
Taylor Swift – Singer/ Songwriter*

*"Every time you wake up and ask yourself
(what good things am I going to do today?)
Remember that when the sun goes down at sunset,
it will take a part of your life with it."
Indian Proverb*

*"No act of kindness,
no matter how small, is ever wasted."
Aesop - Greek Storyteller*

*"Sometimes when we are generous in small,
barely detectable ways,
it can change someone else's life forever."
Margaret Cho - Author & Actress*

Chapter 8 - CRAYONS AND PAINTS

Part 1 - For Your Child

APPRECIATING BEAUTY

*"While we try to teach our children all about life,
our children teach us what life is all about."*
Angela Schwindt - Home Schooling Mum & Unicycle Team Coach

Across the vast spectrum of colour from shimmering gold and burnt orange to scarlet, vibrant green and passionate purple your child creates a stunning picture, a visual masterpiece, a radiant rainbow of adventure in colour. Whether it's colouring between the lines or creating their own shapes and boundaries, paints and crayons provide endless hours of enjoyment.

*"There are no seven wonders of the world in the eyes of a child.
There are seven million."*
Walt Streightiff - Author

Colour your child's world and make it even more ravishing. Encourage them to notice and value nature; it will stay with them forever. Show them all the wondrous shades and hues of life for this is such a glorious planet. You only have to look around at the staggering beauty of a sunset, the ocean, the stars or a tree; nothing man made, could ever be so perfect. Sadly, some people pass through life, virtually on automatic pilot with their eyes open but never actually seeing or appreciating anything. Don't allow your child to become one of them. Make their lives magical, by accentuating the wonder of Mother Earth. Walk on the beach together, build sand castles, feed the ducks, frolic in the surf, gaze up at the stars or savour country walks. Take a moment to appreciate the perfume of a flower, pick strawberries in the summer sun, chase butterflies or sing and play together, for there is nothing more beautiful in the world than the smile and laughter of a child.

*"To be in your children's memories tomorrow,
you have to be in their lives today."*
Barbara Johnson

Part 2 – FOR YOU

BEAUTY WITHIN

*"The more we embrace who we are as people
and rely less on our physical attributes, the more empowered
we become. Beauty shouldn't be so easily designed.
It's limitless."*
Cara Delevingne - Model & Actress

So what makes a woman beautiful, her eyes, her hair, her skin? Though everyone wants to be beautiful, very few women are ever happy about their looks.

*"I think all women go through periods where
we hate this about ourselves, we don't like that.
It's great to get to a place where you dismiss
anything you're worried about. I find flaws attractive."*
Angelina Jolie - Film Actress. Goodwill Ambassador for
UN Refugee Agency

Realistically, every person in the world has 'flaws' but these so called flaws are what actually make us unique. Unfortunately for many women, their whole self-image is totally dependent on the way they look or the size they are. These women are so wrapped up in their 'flaws', dwelling whole heartedly on them, desperately striving to be 'perfect', that they don't even realize in reality 'perfection' doesn't exist. Beauty is always subjective and in the eye of the beholder, for what one person perceives as 'perfect' or beautiful, someone else does not. The truth is you are perfect already, for no one in the whole world looks or is quite like you. No one has your eyes, your face, your hair, your smile, your soul, or the very essence of your unique beauty.

In future, instead of comparing yourself negatively against the media's unrealistic and sometimes rather unattractive and unhealthy looking ideals, concentrate instead on being the very best *you* that you can be. If you're unsatisfied with your weight, lose some. Want another hair colour? Change it. Accept there is nothing about you that is wrong. Indeed, your body, no matter how large, small or in-between is quite literally, the most magnificent creation ever to grace the earth. Be thankful for your sight, your hearing, your incredible ability to run, move think and speak. Feel gratitude, as both your body and mind are truly priceless gifts, gifts that should never be taken for granted.

*"Confidence is the only key. I know a lot of people
who aren't traditionally 'beautiful'
Not symmetrical or perfect- bodied or perfect-skinned.
But none of that matters, because all that shines through
is their confidence, humour and comfort with themselves.
I can't think of any representation of beauty
than someone who is unafraid of herself."*
Emma Stone - Actress

Some females positively exude confidence and both men and women alike are drawn to them in their droves, yet often feature by feature these charismatic femme fatales are far from beautiful, like legendary Cleopatra, sultry Sophia Loren or a whole list of stunning women including Barbra Streisand and the fantastically unique, Grace Jones. Though confident women are aware of their flaws, they totally accept themselves and wouldn't dream of changing. They are perfectly fine, having too much fun just the way they are, the way *you* should be too. In truth, the secret to being beautiful, is quite simply feeling beautiful. Liking and appreciating yourself for the woman you are, for nothing is sexier or more attractive than confidence.

> *"Feeling comfortable in my own skin*
> *makes me feel confident."*
> *Jess Glynne - Singer, Songwriter*

To become more confident, one must first have an idea of the kind of person you'd like to be, for confidence, like self–esteem is simply a learned behavior, it is not inherited.

> *"Everybody looks in the mirror and is like,*
> *I wonder why her eyes are huge and mine are smaller.*
> *But I realized that if you're lucky enough to be different*
> *from everybody else, don't change."*
> *Taylor Swift - Singer & Songwriter*

A confident woman likes and is at ease with herself and makes others feel comfortable around her. She is warm, decisive and genuine and knows what she wants. She thinks positively and will never put others down, in order to make herself feel good. She acknowledges and accepts both her good and bad points and doesn't mind others knowing about them too.

But a person lacking in confidence may frequently feel awkward, worthless, anxious or embarrassed. They may well hate their looks, be rash or indecisive, frequently procrastinate or feel in awe of confident people, dreading parties or get-togethers, regularly avoiding social contact or backing out of dates or rendezvous at the last minute, offering some feeble excuse, then subsequently shutting themselves off from every one, and possibly comfort eating. This usually results in them loathing themselves even more and isolating themselves even further, so they once again comfort eat to hide their loneliness, thus this perverse, unhappy merry-go-round continues. If they would only stop and take the time to change themselves and their thoughts, they could end that miserable and destructive cycle and actually take part in and enjoy their lives, for as their confidence develops, so too will their life. Suddenly their entire world will become so much more positive and exciting. We're only here once, why waste that precious time lurking in the shadows, when you could be living your life, basking in the sunlight?

> *"I really do believe that being naturally beautiful is what is inside and what shines through."*
> Penny Lancaster - Model, Photographer

Ten Steps for Improving Your Self–Confidence.
Following are ten proven steps for building and improving your self-confidence.

Step 1 - Think about someone in particular, a sports or business person, teacher, entrepreneur, movie star, fashion icon, or journalist whose looks and confidence you admire and begin to mirror some of their conduct and mannerisms. Don't ever attempt to become that person but focus on some of the admirable characteristics that have made them so unique, alluring and successful; traits that will set you on the road to discovering your own self-confidence and fulfillment.

Step 2 - Always retain a good sense of humour. Be positive, smile more when you meet and greet people or at life in general. People love being around happy people and the more you smile, the happier you'll feel. Shake people's hands with confidence, instead of hesitantly offering a weak handshake. Truly, who wants to feel like they're shaking hands with a piece of limp lettuce? That gesture alone conveys more than a zillion words ever could, about your character. Instead stand proud. Nothing reflects your confidence more than your eyes and your body language, no matter what words may come out of your mouth. If you shuffle nervously, appear taut or uptight, or keep you head down and avoid eye contact, people will have you sussed in a heartbeat, for your body language will shout volumes; volumes much louder than your voice. The way you move has a huge impact on your confidence. Walk tall with your head up and your shoulders back, as though you are important, for you are. Let your body language reflect that.

Step 3 - Focus on the things you *can* do rather than what you can't. You've already accomplished loads in your life. If you can't think of any, sit down with a piece of paper until you've jotted some things down. Everyone, even you, has accomplished something. Chances are, you're going to accomplish even more great things, in the future.

"But enough about me, let's talk about you.
What do you think of me? ('Beaches' – The Movie)
Bette Midler - Singer, Actress & Producer

Step 4 - Become a good conversationalist and *listen*. People love talking about their favourite subject, themselves. Don't interrupt, but look them in the eye and be enthused about their stories. If you are stuck for something to chat about, introduce such topics as films, business, current affairs, travel, holidays, family, jobs, studies, books, music or hobbies or one of the most interesting subjects of all politics, even Brexit!

Step 5 - Learn from the past. Don't beat yourself up, we've all made mistakes, how else do you grow? Anyone who hasn't erred hasn't really lived. Just avoid making the same old ones in the future. After all, it's from our errors that we learn.

"I've realized that I am who I am and that is it.
Like it or lump it.
I'm not around to please anyone anymore
and it's a huge relief."
Kristin Scott Thomas – Actress, Stage & Screen

Step 6 - Break the habit of trying to please all of the people all of the time. Realistically, it just isn't possible and you'll end up running yourself ragged, chasing your tail trying to make others happy and becoming utterly miserable in the process. Learn how to say 'no'. Don't be scared, for there is nothing to be afraid of. It really is that easy. After you've said 'no' once, they'll be no going back. People will also respect you, as in all honesty, no one admires or reveres a doormat.

Step 7 - Pamper yourself. Buy some fabulous new clothes, have an extra special day or weekend away, or simply get a facial. Just like kids, treats make you feel good and are always a great boost to your soul. If money's tight, watch an incredible film, have an impromptu picnic or savour a glass of inexpensive bubbly.

"Chance favours the prepared mind.
The more you practice, the luckier you become."
Richard Branson - Businessman, Author & Philanthropist

Step 8 - In your professional life, be prepared for meetings and interviews, you'll come across as a lot more relaxed, professional and in control. It'll also be much less stressful. Having said that, don't forget, some of life's most treasured moments and opportunities are born from spontaneity.

Step 9 - Play to your strengths. If there are any areas that you'd like to improve, make a mental note to put a plan in place, to do so. Know what you're good at, then utilize your talents, to the max.

Step 10 - Like, believe in and respect yourself. Enjoy your own company, set your goals and pursue your dreams. Have fun and discover your own personal sense of style and beauty. Recognize what makes you unique. Be bold and celebrate those differences.

"There's only one of you, so why would you want to look like everyone else? Why would you want to have the same hairstyle as everyone else and have the same opinions as everybody else?"
Adele - Singer & Songwriter

    Realize you are exquisite, unparalleled and probably stunning already, maybe you simply hadn't noticed, for you were too busy looking at or admiring others. Accept the features you have, and make the most of them. If you're fed up with your style or lack of it, book a free make up session at a local department store or scour the fashion magazines and books for new looks and ideas that you would like to experiment with. Read positive thinking, self-help books, or biographies about successful people to inspire you and improve your self-confidence. Then learn to feel like the most special woman that you are, for if you believe it, others will too which in turn will re-enforce your own beliefs. Accept that the world is full of beautiful people, one of which is *you*.

FAMOUS LAST WORDS

For Your Child

*"Each day of our lives,
we make deposits in the memory banks
of our children."
Charles Swindoll – U.S. Pastor*

*"Children see magic, because they look for it."
Christopher Moore - Writer*

For You

*"You really have to look inside and find your inner
strength and say "I'm proud of what I am and who I am
and I'm just going to be myself"."
Mariah Carey - Singer/Songwriter, Producer*

*"Show me a person who has never made a mistake and
I'll show you someone who has never achieved much."
Joan Collins - Actress & Author*

*"I'm not going to change my teeth or get a nose job.
That manufactured perfection does nothing for me."
Rosie Huntington-Whiteley - Model, Actress &
Designer*

*"Women are so unforgiving of themselves.
We don't recognize our own beauty because
we're too busy comparing ourselves to other people."
Katy Perry - Singer/Songwriter*

*"If you're comfortable with yourself, then it's sexy."
Scarlett Johansson - Actress & Singer*

*"You don't have to be skinny or beautiful.
Beauty is the size of your heart.
Not the size of your jeans. Confidence is sexy!"
Hplyrikz*

*"Beauty begins the moment
you decide to be yourself."
Coco Chanel - Fashion Designer, Founder of
Chanel*

*"I had to grow to love my body.
I did not have a good self–image at first.
Finally, it occurred to me, I'm either going to love me
or hate me. And I chose to love my self.
Then everything kind of sprung from there.
Things I thought weren't attractive became sexy.
Confidence makes you sexy".
Queen Latifah – Singer, Actress & Producer*

Chapter 9 - BUILDING BLOCKS

Part 1 - For Your Child

THE VALUE OF MONEY

"Play is our brain's favourite way of learning."
Diane Ackerman - Poet & Essayist

It's fun building structures, watching as your child's tiny fingers carefully balance one colourful block on top of the next. From these solid foundations all manner of wonderful edifices can be made, maybe a castle or even a tower. Kids learn that if a foundation is strong, the structure will never buckle, cave in or come crashing down.

If you apply that same logic to finances, you'll be teaching your kids an invaluable lesson and setting them up for a financially secure future ahead. As all children are curious about the mysteries of money, introduce them to it as soon as they can count. Familiarize them with both coins and notes and help them to understand its value. When you go shopping explain to your child how much things cost.

Giving regular pocket money is a great idea, as it provides kids with a sense of independence and excitement, besides giving them control over how their cash is spent and how to manage money. Agree on a fixed amount each week, to be increased yearly on their birthday. As your child grows older, you can add extra top up's and bonuses for chores around the house or getting jobs done, or simply for them being such a great kid. Rewards are not just for what they do, but for who they are.

"The easiest way to teach children the value of money, is to borrow some from them."
Anon

Coins and Fairy Godmothers

Let them count their money and coins as often as they please. Encourage your children to save by investing in a fun looking 'money bank'. If a child wants to buy an item, ask if they are sure that is what they want, or if they would like to save up their money and buy something even bigger later on? Through this a child begins to understand money and the value of their purchase. If their heart is set on something, let them make their own decision and spend their money exactly how they wish. If they manage to accumulate enough, give them a little extra as a reward for their achievement.

As children were advised years ago that money doesn't grow on trees, they should now be taught, that it doesn't miraculously appear out of cash machines either. Explain that when you pay for purchases using a Debit or Credit Card, you must either already have the money in the bank to cover the items, or you are in fact 'borrowing' the money which will shortly have to be repaid. Emphasize that there is not a prosperous fairy godmother out there, supplying endless amounts of cash.

Part 2 - FOR YOU

FINANCIAL FREEDOM

*"Money is better than poverty,
if only for financial reasons."*
Woody Allen - Film Director, Writer, Actor & Playwright

*"Too many people spend money they haven't earned,
to buy things they don't want, to impress people they don't like."*
Will Rogers - Actor, Cowboy & Humourist

Achieving financial freedom is a major goal for most of us but sadly, apart from winning the lottery, many of us find ourselves drowning in a financial quagmire of which we have no idea how to escape. Debts mount up, bills and credit cards go unpaid and stress and anxiety kick in, as you borrow from Peter to pay Paul. It's a miserable catch 22 situation. You're broke, so you borrow more money, which lands you deeper in debt, so you borrow even more. Now is the time to stop that appalling situation from spiraling out of control and producing even more debt.

> *"Without action, the best intentions in the world are nothing more than that: intentions."*
> Jordan Belfort - Stockbroker, Author, *'The Wolf of Wall Street'*

Sadly, debt can so easily escalate out of hand, especially with the outrageous interest rates that Pay Day loans demand, where you end up forever paying off the interest and never the capital sum, the debt seemingly growing impossible to repay. But help really is at hand, for there are a myriad of effective ways to get back on that road to financial stability, all you need is commitment. The first thing to do is plan a budget. Everyone has an income and fixed monthly expenses such as rent/mortgage, utilities, phone bills, food etc. Sit down and itemize every incoming and outgoing expenditure that you can think of, then add in all those other elusive hidden categories such as meals out, coffee shops, school trips, clothes and magazines. It's vital each month that you spend less than the amount coming in, but how can you possibly live within your means, if you haven't a clue what your means are?

If you find your expenses are higher than your income, then you need to take action. Don't bury your head in the sand, hoping that the problem will miraculously disappear. It won't, quite the reverse, for the longer you ignore it, the worse it will become. Acting now will make your situation so much less stressful and doable.

Nine Simple Ways to Economize

1. From today cut back on any and all unnecessary spending, for example, instead of buying expensive new toys, consider buying fewer and swapping them with friends and family. Kids quickly grow out of toys but have great fun playing with new ones. Additionally, check out the fantastic Toy Libraries that are available in most towns. For a nominal amount you can take a variety of toys home, which can be exchanged every week or so;

some of the libraries even include larger toys, suitable for parties. Ask at your local library or check on line for details.

2. Buy books and toys at second hand shops, you really can pick up some great bargains with superb children books, selling for as little as 10p or 20p. Indulge in your local library and take home a fabulous array of books, completely free of charge.

3. Pass on and swap good quality children's clothes with friends etc.

4. Plan weekly meals before your trip to the supermarket. Never shop when you're hungry and buy only fruit and vegetables that are in season. Try supermarket value or generic brands that are inexpensive but generally just as good as major branded items, you'll be astounded at how much you save. Drink tap water as opposed to bottled and avoid buying lunches or food out substitute instead with your own packed lunch.

5. Ditch luxuries that you can ill afford such as cable or satellite T.V. especially with so many Free view channels available. When you go to the movies, opt for off peak or discount times. Watch for reduced admission prices or even free promotional offers to sports events, clubs and local festivities and remember most museums and art galleries are also free. Look for activities that are complimentary or don't cost the earth, such as cycling, a ramble or an inexpensive picnic.

6. Consider switching to a pay as you go mobile, instead of having the added expense of a home phone complete with installation and rental charges. They are frequently cheaper than a contract and give you a huge incentive to phone less.

7. Keep track of your finances and pay for purchases with cash instead of a credit card. You might reconsider whether that purchase or item really is a necessity.

8. Avoid penalty bank charges, pay loans off as quickly as possible and budget monthly so you are able to pay bills on a timely basis. If possible, try to save a little money, on a regular or semi-regular basis.

9. Study or retrain for a new job that pays more in the long run, or put that secret business idea into practice. There are stacks of

books available from both book shops and libraries to show you how to do just that; plus, with the internet, it's possible to promote your business, absolutely free.

> *"He is rich or poor according to what he is,
> not according to what he has."*
> Henry Ward Beecher - Social Reformer & Abolitionist

If you are currently drowning in a sea of debt and have no idea what to do, don't panic for there really is a life raft out there for you and it's literally a phone call away. Simply take the first step and contact a free helpline such as the National Debt line on 0808 808 4000 (nationaldebtline.org) which can help in all matters of debt and finance or Stepchange.org - a nonprofit credit counseling service on 0800 138 1111. It could be the best call you'll ever make. These friendly and efficient people are there to help and help they do, providing an outstanding service. What you may feel is an insurmountable problem is not, for they will kindly and efficiently organize a budget for you, so you'll be able to survive and live within your means on a reasonable and acceptable amount of money, while still paying off your debts, even if you can only manage a few pounds a week. You'll finally be free of those intimidating and incessant phone calls and or threatening letters, giving you the space and peace of mind to financially get back on your feet, so one day, hopefully in the not too distant future, all your outstanding debts will be cleared.

Alternately, contact your local Citizens Advice Bureau, many of whom provide confidential and independent advice on how to deal with your debts. Take a deep breath and make the call. Remember, you are not alone. Help is truly a phone call away.

> *"My last credit bill was so big, before I opened it,
> I actually heard a drum roll."*
> Rita Rudner - Comedienne, Writer & Actress

No matter how overwhelming it may seem, with the proper help and advice, all debt is manageable, for it's never too late to get your finances and life back on track. Don't passively sit back hoping your ship may one day come in. What if it doesn't? Act now and steer yourself towards a happier and more financially secure future. For the first time in probably a long time, you'll be able to look at a new horizon, debt free, solvent and able to consider a new and exciting future. Go for it. Stop worrying. Become your own best friend, by getting that much needed help, today.

FAMOUS LAST WORDS

For Your Child

"Children are our most valuable resource."
Herbert Hoover - 31st U.S. President

For You

*"I'm living so far beyond my income that
we might almost be said to be living apart."
Saki - Writer*

*"Credit buying is much like being drunk.
The buzz happens immediately and gives you a lift,
the hangover comes the day after."
Joyce Brothers - U S Psychologist & TV Personality*

*"People say that money is not the key to happiness,
but I always figured that if you have enough money,
you can have a key made."
Joan Rivers - Comedienne, Producer & TV Host*

*"A bank is a place that will lend you money
if you can prove that you don't need it."
Bob Hope – Comedian, Actor & Humanitarian*

*"You must gain control over your money
or the lack of it will forever control you."
Dave Ramsey - Radio Show Host/Businessman*

*"A simple fact that is hard to learn,
is that the time to save money, is when you have some."
Joe Moore*

Chapter 10 - WENDYHOUSE

Part 1 - For Your Child

TANTRUMS AND BULLIES

*"The real menace in dealing with a five-year-old
is that in no time at all,
you begin to sound like a five-year-old."*
Joan Kerr – 'Please Don't Eat the Daisies' 1957

*"Children seldom misquote. In fact, they usually repeat
word for word what you shouldn't have said."*
Unknown

Children adore playing in Wendy houses, pretending it's their house and re-enacting scenes they either witnessed or experienced. Once again, as always *you* are their example and as sure as day follows night, they will copy both your good and bad actions, your anger and hostility, as well as your kindness and love. It's imperative therefore, to teach by example. If you yell or threaten, you'll exhibit the exact behavior that you want to discourage. Seeing you red-faced and screaming and unable to control your anger will not teach kids how to control theirs. But flip the coin and demonstrate care and respect, your children will quickly follow suit.

Kids need our love and protection not our punishment and abuse. It's far better to discipline a child and teach right from wrong, than to punish. Obviously, it's a parent's choice, but smacking children definitely doesn't guarantee acceptable conduct, quite the reverse. In many ways it shows kids that hitting is a suitable way of solving a problem, when in reality, nobody has the right to hit or smack anyone, either in the home or outside, including a child. Smacking doesn't demonstrate why their actions were wrong and what lessons should be learned. Indeed, sometimes children's misbehavior is simply a mistake in judgment, therefore the penalty should relate to that behavior i.e. if a young child makes a mess he or she should help clean it up. Treat children properly and they in turn will treat you the same way. Don't ever ignore them, jerk them around, or be intimidating but deal with their behavior in a fair, firm and constructive way.

*"When my kids become wild and unruly,
I use a nice safe playpen.
When they're finished, I climb out."*
Erma Bombeck - Humourist & Author

The Dreaded Temper Tantrum

*"Everything I thought I'd hate about having children –
the crying, the screaming – nothing fazes me.
I love it all, and it's relaxed me."*
Elton John - Singer, Pianist & Composer

We've probably all experienced the dreaded temper tantrum. Next time, instead of losing your cool, take time out, count to ten and realize your child does not *enjoy* feeling this way. If your toddler looks as though he's about to erupt, distract him with a toy, picture or any other interesting object. With any luck, in a moment or two, the dreaded outburst will have passed.

If your child *does* experience a full blown tantrum, remember the most important thing any parent can do is to stay calm, empathize and communicate with the child, then figure out exactly what you want to accomplish ie. to calm your child down and quickly rectify the situation. Get down to your child's level and tell them you understand that they're angry or upset. Ask them what's making them feel this way, then listen to their response. Don't assume you know what it is. Show them that you love them and are concerned. Often, in public, an embarrassed parent will revert to ignoring the child, but in this situation, if anyone should be ignored, it's the people around you, not your child. Never belittle, shout at, or in any way, mishandle your child. Don't ever allow your toddler to feel they're being ignored, or even worse, punished for their melt down. Remember, the child hasn't purposely elected to feel this way. This is not a personal vendetta or attack against you. Though it may not be fun for the parent, it's even worse for your child. At all times, sympathize, communicate, cuddle and support your toddler. When he stops for breath, tell him gently that you love him and if he wishes he can come and look at a toy or book with you, or maybe one of his favourite things you've brought along for just such an emergency, something you know will instantly grab his attention. Stay very close to your child but focus your attention on that something else. Encourage him several times, to come and look at it with you, tell him that there are some fabulous pictures that you know he'll love. Then wait patiently till the tirade is over and you hear the sound of his tiny footsteps approaching.

"That best academy, a mother's knee."
James Russell Lowell - Poet, Diplomat & Satirist

If a toddler is naughty at home, either remove their privileges such as TV or simply revert to 'time-out'. Alternatively, ask your child to sit on your knee, as you need to have a word with her. Tell her in a quiet but serious voice that you know she is good girl but what she did was not very nice and that you didn't expect that from her. Tell her why it was unacceptable and agree between you that she won't do it again. Hug and tell her you love her, then carry on with your day and forget it. Don't let those few unhappy moments hang around and spoil the day. Having these little chats will make both your lives so much easier and will set the groundwork for future conduct.

"The word "no" carries a lot more meaning when spoken by a parent who also knows how to say "yes"."
Joyce Maynard - Author & Teacher

When you go shopping, tell her before you leave whether it's a 'Buying' or 'Looking' day - always agree on this before you set off. On 'Buying' days she can select a small toy or book and a few sweets. On 'Looking' days she can look at books, or play with or handle any of the toys but no purchases are made. If she wants sweeties while you are out, tell her that you'll shortly be going for a drink and maybe she can select a small cake for the two of you to enjoy. Explain that having sweets every day is not good for her and today, as agreed, is a 'Looking' day but that the next time you go shopping, she can choose something nice. Then, distract her with something else. Don't simply say "because I said so". An explanation helps her distinguish right from wrong, rather than perceiving rules as mandatory. If your child sees something really special that she'd had her heart set on, maybe buy it as a special treat.

Be consistent. Create ground rules but keep them to a minimum. If you tell her one day that she can't jump on furniture, don't allow her to do it the next. Rules are rules and limits must be set and adhered to, otherwise your child will get confused and end up being 'naughty 'when it really wasn't her fault. If it's a minor issue, sometimes let her have her own way i.e. if she wants to continue playing for an extra ten or fifteen minutes, so be it. Always allow your child to disengage from playing some fun activity with a five-minute, then a two-minute time call. Expecting a child to stop what they are doing immediately, when they're in the midst of having fun and playing a fabulous game, will almost certainly end in tears.

"A person's a person, no matter how small."
Dr Seuss - Writer & Cartoonist of Children's Books

A child is not an adult, they are only tiny and as such, are still learning and growing and should be treated accordingly. Encourage honesty and manners but explain that conduct such as hitting, shoving, name-calling, throwing or breaking things, will never be tolerated. If your child is het up, listen and converse with her rather than arguing. Discussion can quickly diffuse any situation and often the feeling of being understood, is all a kid needs.

Most children at some time or another have been teased but if that teasing becomes hurtful, cruel or constant, then it crosses the line into bullying and has to be stopped. Bullying should never be tolerated and must be dealt with instantly. A self-assured child who is able to fight back or stand up for themselves, will probably be left alone, as bullies are often cowards who would never mess with kids that are equally strong or confident, always seeking out a child who appears to be less self-assured and more vulnerable. If there is the slightest chink in a kid's armour, bullies will detect and exploit it. Often the first step in their attack or onslaught is to separate that child from their friends or the rest of the crowd, following the principle of "divide and conquer". Bullies often appear brave when there is just one victim and they are part of a crowd, needing and adopting the mentality of a pack, to make them feel tough. But often when they are segregated and on their own, the bravado rapidly disappears, leaving them as frightened and intimidated as anyone else.

Signs of Bullying
There are a number of signs a parent can detect, to check if a child is being bullied, such as….
1. A fear of walking to and from school alone, or catching the school bus.
2. An unwillingness to attend school i.e. feeling sick in the mornings or playing truant. Acting withdrawn and/or eating and sleeping poorly.
3. Noticing your child is upset, after using the Internet.
4. Finding your child's books, property or clothes either mysteriously damaged, destroyed or missing.
5. Having your kids arrive home hungrier than usual, possibly after they have been forced, to hand over their lunch money. Bullying can turn a simple lunch time into a nightmare and can be done in a variety of ways for example:

Physical Bullying – Pushing, shoving, punching, spitting, kicking and isolating.
Verbal Bullying – Name calling, threats or having vicious gossip or rumours spread about them, including cyber-bullying i.e. Web based attacks and/or nasty, slanderous and frightening text messages.

None of these should ever be tolerated, not for a moment, for no one deserves to be bullied. At its worse, bullying can culminate in remorseless threats or actual acts of violence, with someone getting seriously hurt. Tragically, some young victims have felt so desperate, they have even taken their own lives. It's critical then to take any form of bullying seriously and not just brush it aside because you don't know how to, or are too embarrassed to deal with it, worried that you'll be perceived by others as over reacting.

> *"If we don't stand up for children,
> then we don't stand for much."*
> Marian Wright Edelman - Children's Activist

Effective Steps
Following are five proven steps parents can take, to help prevent bullying.

1. Sign your kids up for a course in self-defense to boost their confidence, providing of course your children are in agreement.
2. Invite other kids over, so your child develops a wide and strong circle of friends.
3. Become a constant presence at his or her school, supporting your child in their various activities.
4. If possible escort or drive your child to and fro school and other places.
5. Set the privacy setting and monitor your child's internet access.

> *I tell them (her children) that whenever they are feeling
> sad or difficult they must always try to talk about it.
> I ask them to always come to me and tell me what
> is going on in their lives. I tell them they
> should never keep things bottled up."*
> Monica Bellucci - Actress

If you have any suspicions regarding bullying and your child hasn't confided in you, it's imperative that you talk and talk *now*, for children are sometimes too scared to open up, in case the bully finds out and hurts them even worse. They may also assume for some awful reason, that their parents won't believe them or do anything about it, or will simply tell them to fight back, when they are clearly too terrified, to do so.

If your child tells you they *are* being bullied, praise them for being brave enough to talk about it, then assure them of your protection. Let them vent their feelings but don't agree to keep it a secret. No child should be silent when they are being tormented or hurt. Sometimes, if you know the bullies' parents, a discreet word with them and their child is all that is needed. Clarify the fact that neither you nor your child, will tolerate the situation also, that the other child would not want the same kind of treatment, subsequently this behavior must cease. If the bullying persists, see their teacher or the Head of school immediately. He or she will then act as a mediator between yourselves and the other family. Make your case and be persistent until the bullying has been dealt with and has stopped.

"Bullying happens more than you think.
I was bullied in school and it affected me so much
I decided to be home schooled."
Demi Lavato - Actress, Singer & Songwriter

Though there are lots of resources out there to help you, should you find that, despite all your complaints, for some reason nothing has been done, in fact the situation has escalated, then another course of action must be taken. If the bullying has become even worse and your child is genuinely scared of going to school, then maybe you should either change schools or consider home-schooling.

Nowadays there are countless small and excellent groups, where the kids all know and like each other and the parents share the responsibility of teaching or ferrying the children to and fro lessons and activities. Home schooling can be a great way to learn, providing the child is socializing and learning with children of a similar age and not being isolated, which, in turn, could rapidly cause its own additional problems. Back within a happy and safe environment, confidence can be rebuilt and children can excel. Whatever measures are required, your main concern should always be the safety and well-being of your child. Like a lioness protecting her cubs, fight for your child. Their welfare must be your number one priority.

Part 2 - FOR YOU

BULLYING, ARGUMENTS AND CONFLICTS

*"Group conformity scares the pants off me because it's so
Often a prelude to cruelty towards anyone who doesn't
want to – or can't – join the big parade."*
Bette Midler - Singer, Actress & Comedienne

*"Bullying consists of the least competent,
most aggressive employee projecting their incompetence
on to the least aggressive, most competent employee
and winning. Bullies thrive wherever authority is weak."*
Tim Field - Anti-Bullying Activist

According to an analysis in 2015 by the conciliation service ACAS, workplace bullying is on the rise in Britain, costing the economy a whopping £18bn. Unfortunately, many of its victims are too afraid to speak up but bullying should never be tolerated. Not only can it cause extreme stress and anxiety but it can also have severe long term effects on a person's physical and mental health, some sufferers even contemplating suicide. Bullying is more likely to affect either minority ethnic workers, women in male-dominated jobs, disabled workers, or gay and transgender people, with horrific incidents including humiliation, ostracism and verbal or physical abuse.

> *"Workplace bullying, in any form, is bad for business.*
> *It destroys teamwork, commitment and morale."*
> Tony Morgan - Chief Executive. The Industrial Society

If you have been a victim, don't suffer in silence but report it immediately. Insist your complaint is taken seriously and dealt with, with the utmost vigour and discretion. Companies must acknowledge both the problems and consequences that bullying presents, adopting a zero tolerance policy, by putting the care and wellbeing of their staff, above everything else. After all, without their workers, their businesses would quite literally collapse.

Disagreements Are Natural

> *"My parents only had one argument in 45 years.*
> *It lasted 43 years."*
> Cathy Ladman – Comedienne/ T.V. Writer & Actress

It's a fact, even within the closest of families, conflicts or differences of opinion occur, for they are part of everyday life. Though family disagreements are natural, it's often how they are handled that can cause problems, especially in front of young children. Sometimes youngsters feel so anxious and upset when their parents argue, like their whole world is caving in, that they literally shout out their own nonsense words in order to drown out their parent's anger. But confrontation is normal. Show me a family that doesn't have the occasional row and I'll show you a family who may not stick together that long. Believe it or not, there really is a right and healthy way to argue in front of kids. How else will they learn the proper way to negotiate and resolve a conflict, if no one ever teaches them?

If there *is* a family argument, and your children happen to be present, try to observe the following.

1. Firstly, Never Bicker about Your Children - in their presence. This is vital, for damaging things may be said and heard, that can never be taken back but may certainly be retained by your child, long after the argument has finished. During a conflict, never use your child as a weapon against each other, as though they were some insensitive package that you could chuck back and forth, having no regard for the damage or hurt you are causing them.

2. Stay in the Present
Avoid dragging up old issues, especially if you've no idea how to resolve them. Arguing endlessly about the same topics over and over again and never finding a compromise, helps no one. What on earth's the point? It's just upsetting for everyone and will no doubt escalate into a full blown row that so easily could have been avoided.

3. Steer Clear of Intensely Intimate or Private affairs
Personal problems should only be discussed behind closed doors. Avoid fighting over money, debt or financial affairs in front of very young children, if you're unable to communicate in a courteous and civilized way. They won't understand what you are shouting about and will find the whole ordeal frightening and unsettling. Don't name call, criticize, belittle or demean your partner or spouse, or argue with the sole intention of hurting them, competing with each other to see who can be the most spiteful. It's destructive for you, it's lethal for your relationship and it's a nightmare for your kids.

> *"Always keep your words soft and sweet,*
> *just in case you have to eat them."*
> Anonymous

Fighting Fair – 5 'Ground Rules'

> *"Any problem, big or small, within a family,*
> *always seems to start with bad communication.*
> *Someone isn't listening."*
> Emma Thompson - Actress & Screenwriter

Following are 5 guidelines to effectively negotiate your argument, without harming your relationship.

1. Fight fair and avoid degrading language or force.
2. Avoid the endless blame-game or answering a question with another question.
3. Explain how you feel about a particular situation; your desires, disappointments, anger or expectations. Get if off your chest, once and for all, then listen to what your partner is saying, instead of mentally planning your rebuttal.
4. Don't tell your loved one what they should think. It's controlling, presumptuous and insulting.
5. If the argument is spiraling out of control, take time out.

Most of all, remember you love each other. You're not enemies. You're merely experiencing a disagreement. Though it might not be possible in the moment, perhaps when you've both calmed down, you can look for various solutions together, that may actually result in bringing you both even closer.

> *"Lovers quarrels are the renewal of love."*
> 'Andria' – Terrance, Roman Playwright

Show your kids how to sensibly negotiate and resolve a situation, how to give and take and not to sulk, pout or become resentful, if you don't get it all your own way. Don't wallow in disagreements or make snide remarks. When it's over, it's over. Move on.

If an agreement has been made, accept it wholeheartedly or agree to disagree. Afterwards, both parties should feel validated and still very much in love. People who love each other can disagree passionately and yet still remain best friends. Make up, forgive and carry on as normal. Let children see that an argument really isn't the end of the world. Just a simple glitch in the journey of life.

FAMOUS LAST WORDS

For Your Child

"A child will know how to love when they have been loved, but a child who has been hurt, must learn how."
Unknown

"People tend to think that because I'm a Performer and I don't go to a regular high school that I haven't personally been affected by bullies. But it's actually quite the opposite."
Ariana Grande – Singer

Safety and security don't just happen, they are the result of collective consensus and public investment. We owe our children, the most vulnerable citizens in our society, a life free of violence and fear.
Nelson Mandela – Former president of South Africa

For You

"It is better to debate a question without settling it than to settle a question without debating it."
Joseph Joubert - French Moralist & Essayist

"Like all the best families, we have our share of eccentricities, of impetuous and wayward youngsters and of family disagreements."
Queen Elizabeth 11

"The reward for conformity, is that everyone likes you but yourself."
Rita Mae Brown - Writer & Feminist

*"Never be bullied into silence.
Never allow yourself to be made a victim.
Accept no one's definition of your life,
but define yourself."*
Harvey Fierstein - Actor & Playwright

*"Strong people stand up for themselves.
But the strongest people stand up for others."*
Unknown

*"I realized that bullying never has to do with you.
It's the bully who's insecure."*
Shay Mitchell.

*"A woman is like a tea bag – you never know how
strong she is until she gets in hot water."*
Eleanor Roosevelt - Diplomat & Activist

*"Arguments are to be avoided –
they are always vulgar and often convincing."*
Oscar Wilde - Poet & Playwright

Chapter 11 - DRESSING UP

Part 1 - For Your Child

FINDING THEMSELVES

*"Free the child's potential and you
will transform him into the world."*
Maria Montessori - Physician Educator & Philosopher

Besides being enormous fun, dressing up doesn't have to be expensive, it's incredible how a handful of old scarves, hats, feathers, shoes, a remnant or two of fabric, some clunky jewelry and a couple of toy swords can be transformed into the most ravishing costumes.

Dressing up develops confidence and creates a host of wonderful memories. It also gives children a great idea of who they are and what they aspire to be, whether it's an astronaut or a princess, kids love trying other characters on for size to see how they fit.

Youngsters also love imitating those closest to them. Little girls will frequently emulate their mothers, fussing over and taking care of their 'babies'. Conversely, girls may dress up as blood thirsty pirates, whilst boys will festoon themselves with colourful baubles and beads. If this is the case, let them. Don't restrict kids in any way, for children naturally go through phases and enjoy acting out and exploring different male and female persona. Allow them to develop their own style, likes and dislikes, without being laughed at, ridiculed or teased. Let their imagination run free to become whoever they wish, without fear of recrimination. If boys fancy wearing beads, let them. Similarly, if girls want to play with swords and trucks, what on earth's the harm? Restricting them is pointless, as is imposing meaningless boundaries.

"One of the virtues of being very young is that you don't let the facts get in the way of your imagination."
Sam Levenson - Humourist Writer & Journalist

Part 2 - FOR YOU

VISUALIZATION

"Ask for what you want and be prepared to get it."
Maya Angelou - Poet, Singer & Civil Rights Activist

As a matter of course, children generally feel entitled to be given what they ask for but very few adults dare imagine that life will fulfill their dreams, in quite the same way.

*"What the mind can conceive and believe,
it can achieve."*
Napoleon Hill - Author of Motivational Books

When you were a child, which characters did *you* try on? What were you going to be or achieve when you grew up? Looking into the future, did you imagine your future life as it is now? Have you turned out to be the amazing grown up you wanted to be or has your character still room for improvement? Chances are, like most people, there are things about both yourself and your life you'd radically like to change. The wonderful thing is, it really *never is* too late.

Scripting Your Own Life

Suppose, for a moment, that you could script your own life? How would it look? Close your eyes and imagine your future as if it were a film with you in the title role. How would you see yourself? Who would you be? What would be different? Like it or not, your life right now is a reflection of your past thoughts. Unfortunately, most people have a tendency to dwell on or imagine what they don't want, rather more than what they do and end up getting precisely that. From now on take control of your life. Your future does not have to mirror your past; it could be entirely different starting from today, for everything in life begins with a thought, every journey a simple step, like the story of the opening day of Disney World in Orlando, Florida.

> *"A reporter exclaimed to Walt's brother Roy:*
> *"It's too bad Walt didn't live to see this".*
> *Roy, without missing a beat said:*
> *"Walt saw it first, that's why you're seeing it now"."*

Seeing with The Mind's Eye

> *"Whatever you hold in your mind on a consistent basis is exactly what you will experience in your life."*
> Tony Robbins - Author, Life Coach

A vital part of receiving what you desire is visualizing or 'Seeing with the Mind's Eye'. Visualization is, in fact, a huge step towards attaining your dream, for if you can't see or imagine yourself doing or achieving something, how in the world can it happen? Whether we realize it or not, we visualize constantly, either negatively or positively. We visualize or imagine in our mind what we are having for dinner, an exotic holiday we've booked, an upcoming celebration, starting a new job or replaying an argument we had with loved ones. People mentally rehearse scenes, either real or imagined, over and over in their minds. Unfortunately, like self-talk, the pictures or images we conjure up are frequently negative scenarios, such as, unpaid bills, a lack of money, being overweight, feeling unhappy in a relationship or just being totally unfulfilled. And, like your words, what you think about most, is what you ultimately attract. Ruminate about debt and you will attract more debt. Think of yourself as overweight, lazy or ill and that's precisely what you'll become. Thus, the key to improving your life and acquiring your dream is to reprogram those mental images and thoughts, for all change begins in the mind.

"To believe in the things you can see and touch is no belief at all. But to believe in the unseen is both a triumph and a blessing."
Bob Proctor – Speaker, Author & Trainer

Before altering your circumstances, you must first imagine yourself differently. Though it's a simple process, neither physically exhausting or painful, it is still one of the hardest things a person can do, which is precisely why so few people do it.

Understand that if you desire to be slim, healthy or rich you must first begin to visualize or see yourself as that. Naturally it takes effort to do this. Let's be honest, it's much easier to stay with what's familiar and safe, the familiar feels comfortable and, for better or for worse, it gives us a sense of security. We know what to expect. Even if disappoint leads to more disappointment, allowing us to drift from one bad experience to another. But is this really what you want for the rest of your life? If not, have the guts to say *enough*. It's time for a change. You, like everybody else deserve it.

The Art of Visualization – Wealth, Happiness and Success

From now on, allocate several minutes every day, to visualize. Sit quietly in a place where you won't be disturbed. Breathe deeply, close your eyes, take a deep breath in and hold it for a count of 10 then slowly exhale, letting yourself relax as you go. Take another breath, hold it for 10 and again exhale. Feel yourself drift into a comfortable and warm space as your breathing slows down and waves of relaxation flow over you.

Now, in your mind's eye, create a picture of what you want, your ultimate desire, as vividly as you can with colour and sound. Imagine seeing yourself on that movie screen. Project your image on to it, as you visualize yourself, living that incredible dream. Take in the details of the picture and involve all your senses. Really see, hear and feel the experience.

If it's wealth you envisage, stop visualizing yourself as being broke or poor, as this will only perpetuate the situation. One of the secrets of being wealthy is to feel positive about wealth. If you want money, then you must envisage yourself as a person who *is* moneyed. Imagine how you'd feel seeing vast sums of money, deposited into your bank account every day, smiling with delight as you experience all the wonderful things that life has to offer. Maybe you long for an exciting or glamorous career, be it as an actor, writer, business person, teacher, politician, scientist, doctor or lawyer. If so, view yourself as being successful and living that opulent new life.

If you dream of losing weight, concentrate on the size and weight you intend to be, not on what you are or how much you have to lose, for if you think of losing weight, guess what, your thoughts will be answered and you will constantly have to lose weight. Instead, think slim, ditch the scales and stop reinforcing how heavy or overweight you are. If you concentrate instead on being slim and fit, that's exactly what you'll become, as will your thoughts. Subsequently you'll become more active and adopt healthier habits such as eating a balanced and nutritious diet. See yourself as you want to be, with that slender new body. Really feel the emotions you'll feel when you attain your goal, wearing those knock out clothes and receiving those fabulous compliments.

> *"There used to be a huge hole in my life*
> *that I wrote many albums about.*
> *I didn't realise it was a wife-and-daughter*
> *shaped hole. They've plugged that gap.*
> *Everything I do, I do for them now."*
> Robbie Williams - Singer, Songwriter & Entertainer

If you yearn for romance, imagine holding hands, whispering sweet nothings with that someone special, as you watch the sun go down. Visualize how wonderful it will be to have that new lover, mentor, friend and soul mate in your life.

Whatever you want, truly feel and hold the excitement of what you're visualizing. Engage all of your senses. See yourself actually living your dream. Don't worry if it's not a perfect picture. Like everything, visualization takes practice. The more you do, the clearer the images will become. Visualize the identical pictures or scenes for at least 10 to 15 minutes every day, then watch, as the images in your mind, quickly become the pictures of your life.

> *"I would visualize things coming to me.*
> *It would just make me feel better.*
> *Visualization works if you work hard. That's the thing.*
> *You can't just visualize and go eat a sandwich."*
> Jim Carrey - Actor & Comedian

Throughout the day, discard any negative doubts or self-talk that may pop up such as *"this is crazy, it's not going to work, it's taking too long, it's not possible for me to have that. I don't deserve this"*, otherwise you'll be in a horrible stop/start mode, constantly undoing all your good work and never achieving what you want. Don't sabotage all your efforts by carrying damaging or limiting pictures around, of what you *don't* want; they'll simply cancel out and undermine all your great progress.

From today, believe your success is 100% guaranteed and start 'Acting as if' you have already received your desire. Act as though your life is *already* on track and exactly how you pictured it in your dreams, for the more faith you have, the quicker your dreams will materialize. If you want someone to share your future, begin acting as though they are already there, by literally making room for them in your life. Many people begin sleeping on one side of the bed as opposed to the middle, or clearing cupboards or space, for that new person's belongings.

> *"Act as if! Act as if you're a wealthy man,*
> *rich already and then you'll surely become rich.*
> *Act as if you have unmatched confidence and people*
> *will surely have confidence in you.*
> *Act as if you have unmatched experience*
> *and then people will follow your advice.*
> *And act as if you are already a tremendous success*
> *and as sure as I stand here today –*
> *you will become successful."*
> *Jordan Belfort – Author, Speaker & Wolf of Wall Street*

If it's money you want, act as if you already have wealth, by mentally re-affirming that you can easily afford things, no matter what they are, or how much they cost. Trust that you have an endless and constant supply of money, either known or unknown, from a range of reputable sources that is coming to you on a daily basis. From now on, every time you see something that you'd like, be it a car, a house, a life-style, a yacht or a holiday, think to yourself that you *can* afford it, as opposed to you can't. That doesn't mean running up bills or living above your means or in a state of denial, it means thinking differently, and actually seeing yourself as having riches right *now*. Savour the incredible feeling of being able to help others and how good it will make all of you feel, for frequently, the gift of giving and helping those less fortunate, far outweighs the pleasure of receiving.

Go out and sample those expensive perfumes or aftershaves, or try on those gorgeous clothes. Get brochures for that yacht you so secretly hanker for, or test drive that Porsche or car you so fervently desire. Research all those exotic places in the world you've been longing to visit or settle. Contact realtors and actually check out the kind of property you'd love to own or reside in, be it a spectacular country estate, a palatial villa, a stunning apartment or a charming thatched cottage. Imagine yourself standing in the house, really see it and experience the furnishings, the colours, the décor.

> *"I think I never ceased to be grateful of the fact*
> *that I am able to do a job that I really love –*
> *I never got over that."*
> Judy Dench - Stage, Film & TV Actress

To really accelerate the process, show gratitude, for gratitude is unquestionably one of the most important processes of all. By showing gratitude for what you already have, you will instantly attract an abundance of things into your life that will make you feel even more grateful.

> *"I dream pretty big but truly had no idea*
> *my life could be this awesome.*
> *I am the luckiest girl in the world, without question!"*
> Meghan, Duchess of Sussex

Be thankful for the freedoms we have, for our loved ones, smiles and kisses, great health, nature and all its beauty, the opportunities we have, the food we eat, the clean water we drink, books, music, films, travel, museums and theatres. There are a zillion things to be grateful for. Don't ever overlook or undervalue them or take these precious gifts for granted. Many of us are so incredibly fortunate to have them in our lives.

Start trusting, not just in the current images of your life but in the exciting, invisible future that lays ahead. Realize it's time to bring those images and dreams out of the shadows and make them the magnificent reality of your life. Have faith, for the more you believe, the quicker your dreams will materialize. Along the way, be mindful of your self-talk, for how you speak to yourself and your attitude, are both vital to your success. Besides visualizing and 'Acting as if' repeat your positive affirmations at least three times a day with enthusiasm. Reading, feeling, picturing and hearing your dreams, will have a profound effect on your subconscious mind. Do these things on a daily basis and you'll find yourself adopting new behaviors that will both support and reinforce your dreams. Change your thoughts...and you'll very rapidly, change your life.

FAMOUS LAST WORDS

For Your Child

*"Children must be taught how to think,
not what to think."*
Margaret Mead – Cultural Anthropologist

*"Children are great imitators.
So give them something great to imitate."*
Unknown

For You

*"Success is a state of mind.
If you want success,
start thinking of yourself as a success."*
Dr. Joyce Brother - American Psychologist &
Columnist

*"It is never too late
to become what you might have been."*
George Eliot - English Novelist

*"The real power behind whatever success
I have now, was something I found in myself –
something that's in all of us,
I think, a little piece of God,
just waiting to be discovered."*
Tina Turner - Singer, Actress & Author

*"If you can't be content for what you have received,
be thankful for what you have escaped."*
Isaak Walton - Writer

*"I always felt like I could do anything.
That's the main thing people are controlled by!
Thoughts - their perception of themselves!
They're slowed down by their perception of themselves.
If you're taught you can't do anything;
you won't do anything.
I was taught I could do everything.
And I'm Kanye West at age 36."*
Kanye West - Rapper, Singer & Record Producer

"Act as if what you do makes a difference. It does."
William James - Philosopher

*"Losers visualize the penalties of failure
Winners visualize the rewards of success."*
Dr Rob Gilbert - Author

Chapter 11 - JIGSAWS

Part 1 - For Your Child

ACCEPTANCE

*"Allow children to be happy in their own way,
for what better way will they ever find?"*
Mahatma Gandhi - Lawyer & Nationalist

Kids adore making jigsaws, fitting each new fun piece together with anticipation until they have built a complete picture; not only do jigsaws teach them dexterity and patience but when the puzzle's done, it gives them a tremendous sense of achievement. Occasionally if a piece doesn't fit, it may be tossed aside or discarded, but in the end, a kid will generally carry on building until the piece is incorporated within the puzzle, for every single piece, though different, is vital.

   Children are similar to this as they learn to build the enthralling jigsaw that is their life, never forcing pieces or people to fit, merely accepting that, like the pieces of a puzzle, we are all totally different. Most kids are incredibly accepting and open minded, taking other kids on face value. If another child is fun or friendly it doesn't matter whether they are black, white or sky blue with polka dots, for no child is born with prejudice, it like everything else, has to be taught. It's only as children grow older that they learn to become less tolerant; how tragic when it's the diversity of cultures and nationalities that makes this world that much richer.

"Prejudices, it is well known, are most difficult to eradicate from the heart whose soil has never been loosened or fertilized by education; they grow there, firm as weeds among stones."
Charlotte Bronte - Novelist & poet

But tolerance is essential for your child's future, for the adult who is more enlightened and open to difference in this multicultural world, generally experiences greater opportunities in education, business and numerous other aspects of their life. In fact, success in today's world depends on being able to appreciate, adapt and work with others, no matter what their sexual preference, ethnic background, disability, religion or culture. As kids mature, parents should encourage their child's openness by teaching them to respect and learn from others.

"Children learn more from what you are, than what you teach."
Rishika Jain's Inspirations

Cultivating Tolerance in your Kids

"If you as parents cut corners, your children will too. If you lie, they will too. And if parents snigger at racial and gender jokes, another generation will pass on the poison adults still have not had the courage to snuff out."
Marian Wright Edelman - Activist for the Rights of Children

From now on, become aware of the way you refer to others, who are different from yourself. Avoid jokes or demeaning names of dissimilar races, religions or sex that perpetuate stereotypes. They may seem like harmless fun but they are not. And to young ears, they simply undermine everything you've taught.

"There's nothing that can help you understand your beliefs more than trying to explain them to an inquisitive child."
Frank A. Clark - Athlete

Talk to your child about tolerance, answering their questions about differences honestly. Teach them the values you want them to have. Point out that, even in families, people are different but we never try to hurt or belittle each other because of it. Embrace diversity, for very often, it's only similarities that are celebrated i.e. she looks, walks, talks, dresses and plays like us, thus she *is* one of us. Similar seems to represent good whereas dissimilar equates to bad or wrong. Show your child that is not the case and that you appreciate diversity in all its forms.

No child should ever feel inadequate, second best or left secretly wanting to be someone else who appears to be more 'important' or popular. While it's okay to admire others, children should never compare or judge their value as a human being based in relation to some 'norm' such as how rich, good looking or clever they are, for every youngster, in their own right, is priceless.

Emphasize especially with older kids the powerful and often destructive effect social media can have on trying to shape young people's attitudes and beliefs, from Face book, Instagram, and the internet to television and magazines. Monitor your child's books, toys and DVDs. While they're young, be interested in what they're reading or searching on the internet. Tell stories that reflect and give insight into other children's lives. Encourage your child to grow up, lenient and open-minded and to follow in their own liberal footsteps, for parents who demonstrate tolerance in life, send out a very strong and powerful message.

Part 2 - FOR YOU

TOLERANCE

"If you judge people, you have no time to love them."
Mother Teresa - Humanitarian & Nobel Peace Prize Winner

Notice your own attitude, for intolerance manifests itself in very subtle ways. As Martin Luther King, the U.S. Civil Rights Leader stated;

> *"History will have to record that the greatest tragedy of this period of social transition was not the strident clamor of the bad people, but the appalling silence of the good people."*

Many adults are actually unaware they even have prejudice for their feelings, distrusts, fears and suspicions have never been voiced, their thoughts, merely a series of silent apprehensions; things never spoken about or admitted out loud, even to oneself. But prejudice is so often based less on hate or dislike than on fear of the unknown and the fact that it's easier and safer to stay with what they know. But that mindset stops a whole new world of experience from opening up, for the rigid never grow, they simply grow older. Isn't it better to live 10,000 unique days than to live the same day 10,000 times.

*"Prejudice is a great time saver,
you can form opinions
without having to get the facts."*
E B White - Writer

Standing Up for Yourself
Though tolerance includes accepting and treating others the way you yourself would like to be treated, it doesn't mean enduring or excusing any hurtful or aggressive type of behavior. If there's something you're unhappy about, say it. Let others know how you feel, they're not clairvoyant, people can only respond to what and how you communicate. If somebody's taking advantage, tell them. If they're treating you badly, stop them; there's nothing wrong with standing up for yourself rather than allowing others to stamp on your good nature or kindness. It's up to you therefore to get your message across in the most effective way possible.

*"The single biggest problem in communication,
is the illusion that it has taken place."*
George Bernard Shaw – Playwright & Political Activist

As significant as communication is for understanding and tolerance, it appears unfortunately, according to research done with a certain price comparison website, that we are currently becoming a somewhat uncommunicative lot. Incredibly, one person in four actually texts messages to fellow house dwellers, rather than going to speak with them, a huge 9% insisting it's because they don't wish to see the person; which rather beggars the question, if the individual is so dreadful, why on earth are they living together? Astoundingly, one in fourteen people have gone an entire week or more, without speaking face to face with the person they live with preferring again to either send a text or email or use Face book. Isn't it about time we asked ourselves, why we are becoming so insular, when one of the greatest things in life is communication? It seems people want to shut themselves off, much like they did in a handful of bars many years ago in New York, where drinkers sat isolated within their own little screened off cubicle at the bar, drinking their booze. Talk about a fun night out!!

> *"A best friend is like a four leaf clover,
> hard to find and lucky to have."*
> Sarah Jessica Parker - Actress & Producer

From today, try to find the good in people. Frequently, at the start of a new relationship, people tend to look at their friends or partners with tolerance and love, through rose–tinted glasses, only seeing the best in them. However, as time goes by, the opposite happens; those glasses become clouded and cynical, so people switch to focusing on the bad, concentrating solely on the other persons irritating habits or traits. But how would you feel if someone constantly criticized or nit-picked *your* shortcomings or failings, instead of dwelling on your finer points? You'd feel pretty dire, not only about yourself but about the other person too.

Lighten up and accept people's imperfections. We all have them and in truth most people are doing the very best they can. Stop the blame game, it never solves a thing and usually escalates a problem. Forget the 'I'm right, you're wrong mode'. For better or worse, words and hurtful accusations are remembered long after they're said.

In truth, everyone has spats or arguments, its part and parcel of life and healthy relationships; they clear the air and let people know where you stand. To have a permanent and honest relationship and never have one, seems to me to be an enigma. Humans are not saints; neither can we expect ourselves or others to be. Being on your best behavior 24 hours a day, seven days a week is impossible. Arguments are fine, it's just how that argu-

ment is handled that makes the difference. Keep a sense of perspective and avoid stupid arguments about nothing. If you were given only three months to live would you rather waste time fussing and fighting or enjoying happy times with your loved ones? Face it, one day your life is going to end. I promise the one thing you'll never regret is the time you spent saying "I love you" and cherishing precious moments spent together. Like the Prime Minister (Hugh Grant) stated in the movie....
'Love Actually' ...

> *"Before the planes hit the Twin Towers,*
> *as far as I know,*
> *none of the phone calls from the people on board*
> *were messages of hate and revenge –*
> *they were all messages of love."*

Learn to air your grievances, then forget it and move on. Try putting yourself in someone else's shoes and seeing the world from their perspective, it can often work wonders, for frequently a situation or answer, is not as clear cut as you assumed.

> *"A bore is someone who talks,*
> *when you wish him to listen."*
> Ambrose Bierce - Writer & Journalist

Equally, one of the most important talents we as humans can develop, is the art of listening. There's a reason we have only one mouth and two ears. Take the hint, become a good listener, show you're interested in what's happening in the other person's life and that you're concerned. Some people are so wrapped up in themselves, that their fellow conversationalist can barely finish their sentence, before they have quickly drawn breath and are off again about themselves. Needless to say a good conversation should have two parties involved.

Finally, don't try to change people, you didn't choose the friends or partner you are with because of their potential to eventually become the person you wanted them to be. Understand, what makes them tick, accept them for who they are and ensure they accept you too. People have a right to be themselves, who else are they better at being? No one has permission to try and alter someone to fit their idea or mode of their ideal person or child. Trying to change someone is also a waste of time, for realistically, unless the person wants to change, it will never happen. In life, though similarities are important, it's the differences that make us interesting.

FAMOUS LAST WORDS

For Your Child

*"Where did we ever get the crazy idea that,
in order to make children do better,
first we have to make them feel worse?
Think of the last time you felt humiliated
or treated unfairly.
Did you feel like cooperating or doing better?"
Jane Nelson - Author & Child Therapist*

*"Soft is the heart of a child,
take care not to harden it."
Unknown*

For You

*"Most comedy is based on getting a laugh at
somebody else's expense. And I find that that's
just a form of bullying in a major way,
so I want to be an example that you
can be funny and be kind and make people laugh
without hurting somebody else's feelings."
Ellen DeGeneres - Comedienne & TV Host*

*"A gossip is one who talks to you about others;
a bore is one who talks to you about himself;
and a brilliant conversationalist is one
who talks to you, about yourself."
Lisa Kirk - Actress & Singer*

*"Everyone you meet is fighting a battle you
know nothing about. Be kind. Always."
Plato - Athenian Philosopher*

"The test of courage comes when we are in the minority. The test of tolerance comes when we are in the majority".
Ralph W Sockman - Senior Pastor, Christ Church, New York

"Too many girls rush into relationships, because of the fear of being single, Then start making compromises and losing their identity. Don't do that."
Katy Perry - Singer/Songwriter

" "Tolerance is giving to every other human being the right that you claim for yourself."
Robert Green Ingersoll - Writer & Orator

"How you speak of others is more a reflection of you, then it is of them."
Hazel Butterworth

Why does a woman work 10 years to change a man's habits and then complain that he's not the man she married?"
Barbra Streisand - Singer, Film & Theatre Actress

Chapter 13 - ABACUS

Part 1 - For Your Child

GROWING UP TOO FAST

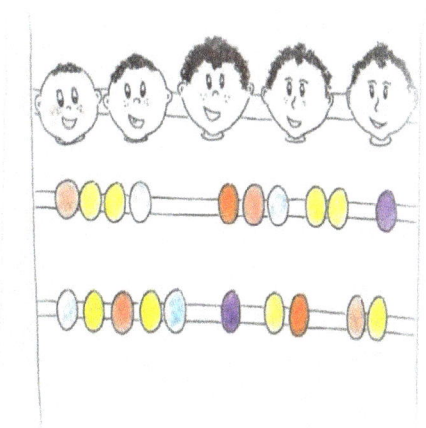

*That's the trouble with the world,
too many people grow up."
Walt Disney - Founder of Disney Co.*

With their colourful counting beads, kids easily understand numbers and functions such as addition, subtraction and multiplication. Young children love numbers and learning how to understand and have fun with them, is an essential skill. It's an incredible concept, even to adults, that everything in this universe is countable, including of course the years.

*"We worry about what a child will become tomorrow
yet we forget that he is someone today."
Anon*

Children seem to grow up *so* quickly, it seems one minute they're in diapers, the next in a school disco. For some absurd reason it's frequently the parents who feel it's cool to fast track their kids through childhood. But is it? Children have all the time in the world to be an adult but only a few short precious years to enjoy silliness, innocence and childhood. You only get one shot at being a kid but the rest of your life to be mature. Why miss out on the fun?

Sometimes it can be the youngsters themselves that strive to look like and behave as adults, as though they've no idea how to be a child. How sad when a nine-year-old has an eating disorder such as Bulimia or wants to know the calorie content of a meal. You only have to look at some of the sexy, ridiculously provocative, fashions aimed at young girls to realize the world is trying to sexualize them much too early and making money at it, while doing so. Many girls believe that wearing makeup, dressing seductively, staying out late or having some sort of love interest, elevates their status in the eyes of their peers.

Shamefully, countless young people are exposed to a cocktail of sex, violence and foul language that used to be relegated only to adult late night viewing. Today it appears almost an expected feature in everyday T.V, especially with some of the more popular programs. Kids can even access atrocious and pornographic sites that populate the internet. But trying to act like adults when they are too young, often leaves kids terribly confused and upset, facing moral dilemmas that are way over their heads, for they are much too young to handle them.

One way to combat this is to encourage your child to read books with positive messages; messages that completely contradict that way of thinking and direct them to a much more wholesome way of life. The huge success of books, such as Harry Potter, proves kids really love reading adventurous, exciting books about other kids and have always done so.

Allow Your Child to Enjoy Being a Kid

> *"You know your children are growing up when they stop asking you where they came from and refuse to tell you where they're going."*
> P.J. O'Rourke - Satirist Journalist & Writer

Interest your children in fun after school activities, such as Drama or Stage school, the school choir, football, basketball, sports clubs, dancing, swimming or martial arts, indeed anything and everything that will keep them from congregating with others and just "hanging out" aimlessly on the streets, where trouble is sure to follow. Ensure they enjoy such a great family life at home, they simply look forward to coming home and relaxing.

Children should be protected and allowed to remain children. If possible, discourage your child from walking to or from school alone especially when tiny, or being left on their own. If they're too young, anything could happen and their safety should not be compromised for a moment. It's our responsibility to provide them with love and protection, every child is entitled to at least that.

Monitor your children's TV and don't allow them to go on websites other than one's that you've already investigated. Definitely avoid chat rooms as, in all reality, anyone or everyone could have access to your child, including a middle aged pedophile posing as a twelve-year-old. Prohibit kids from watching unsuitable DVD's or being exposed to violent or aggressive behavior, for bad language is frightening and teaches them nothing. A kid who grows up seeing cruelty can easily become conditioned to it, resulting in a considerably harder and more dispassionate and colder human being. Like a murder several years ago in America, where a child witness said it was just like watching it on TV but without the music. These days there are a zillion fabulous films for kids to choose from, so there's really no excuse to stick them in front of something unsuitable.

"Children have neither past nor future;
they enjoy the present, which very few of us do."
Jean de la Bruyere - French Essayist & Moralist

Tell your kids how wonderful it is to be a child. Assure them that they actually possess many terrific qualities that some adults, unfortunately lose, including a wonderfully free spirit, curiosity and endless enthusiasm.

Teach kids how to be responsible and when the time is right, how to prepare for adulthood. Till then encourage them to laugh, have fun and *enjoy* being a child. They'll only ever have one childhood!

"The prime purpose of being four
- is to enjoy being four –
of secondary importance
is to prepare for being five."
Jim Trelease - 'The Read Aloud Handbook' 1985

Part 2 – FOR YOU

PROCRASTINATION

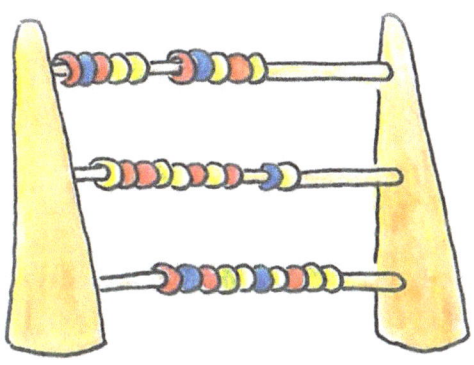

"If it weren't for the last minute, nothing would get done."
Rita Mae Brown - Writer & Activist

As kids have only one childhood, we all have only one life, one that should be lived to the full, not wasted, delayed or postponed. Don't wait for some elusive permission to start living, this is not a rehearsal; this is the real deal. Unlike a relay race, you don't hand the baton over to someone else, for life is yours for the long haul, just make sure you're competing in the right race.

*"Procrastination is hands down,
our favourite form of self-sabotage."*
Alyce P. Cornyn-Selby - Speaker & Author

If you've found yourself putting off important tasks both big and small, you're not alone. Though it's part of human nature, procrastination invariably has devastating consequences. Many people procrastinate their entire life, to such a degree, that it actually robs them of any sort of lifelong achievement. Others constantly put things off in favour of doing something more enjoyable and end up living their life in a kind of guilty twilight zone, knowing they should be pursuing something else and not enjoying what they are doing, then finding themselves panicked or under the gun.

Many people can feel overwhelmed by a task or project and simply not know where or how to begin, or may wait until the time or mood feels right. Either way, when the job is finally complete, it's probably not to the standard it could have been. For others the terrifying fear of failure or success quite literally stops them in their tracks. But it's from these failures we learn. Failures are one of the most important stepping stones we can experience on our road to success. Indeed, a person who's afraid to fail, is afraid to succeed.

Stop Procrastinating...Now!

There are a number of pro-active steps one can take to amend this highly negative and destructive behavior, steps that should be taken, no not tomorrow, or in a little while, but today.

First, figure out exactly the reason *why* you're procrastinating, for in order to overcome or defeat it, you must understand what is making you procrastinate in the first place. There are several reasons why people procrastinate. Maybe you feel helpless in a situation, unable to prioritize or make a decision, perhaps you are easily distracted, have little or no motivation or simply want to rebel in some way against what is expected of you. Once you've figured out the cause, replace all those excuses or negative fears with positive ones. Imagine how great you'll feel when the task is complete, then as the Nike slogan suggests 'just do it'.

Compile a list of the things you've been putting off, from the most to the least important. Identify the unpleasant consequences of not completing that job, then break it up into tiny bite size tasks. By completing each one, you'll feel like you're achieving something, so the chore won't be quite so daunting. Work through the list checking off the items as you go. Seeing the list diminish will give you a massive boost.

Treat yourself after you've completed a particularly arduous or mundane job; the thought of a reward will help keep you focused and inspired. Be realistic. Allow yourself more than adequate time to finish your work. Don't assume that what would in reality take someone else two hours will only take you one. It's better to finish ahead of schedule than leave yourself rushed.

Additionally, stop being a perfectionist, constantly critiquing anything you try, surely that would be enough to stop anyone in their tracks. Recognize that 80% for you, could well be 100% for someone else. Just do the very best you can, and be proud of your achievement.

Living for the Moment

> *"Never look back. If Cinderella had looked back and picked up the shoe, she would never have found her prince."*
> *Selena Gomez - Singer/Songwriter & Producer*

Studies have shown, the happiest people are those who live for the moment and embrace every second of their life. We should all appreciate what we have and plan exciting and fulfilling futures. It's a fact, our future is largely the product and result of what we do today, so get up off your duff and start living *now*. Take responsibility for your actions. If you don't like something about your life, change it. Don't expect others to do it for you. The key to happiness lies within us, not without. If you're unhappy, maybe you've been looking in the wrong place or doing the wrong things. Don't drift unhappily along wasting all those precious years that you can never retrieve, for life really is the most beautiful thing. As the French novelist Colette rued;

*"What a wonderful life I've had.
I only wish I'd realized it sooner."*

If you spend your life looking back over your shoulder regretting past mistakes and lost opportunities, how can you possibly ever see your way ahead? The past is gone, learn from it and press on. Don't for heaven's sake live your life wallowing in it. It's aging, it's negative and it's a complete waste of time, for today really is the first day of the rest of your life. Be sure to make it a great one.

Love your kids, love yourself and love your life. Let your miraculous children show you the wonder that is within every single one of us, as they open up and play with their toys from 'Dolls & Teddies' and the importance of Self-Esteem to 'Bubbles, Balloons & Kites' and shooting for the moon. Watch and learn too, as your child becomes the best and most remarkable person they can be, for unquestionably the teaching, guiding and love of our amazing children, turn us parents into better people. For children truly are, one of the greatest gifts and inspirations, we could ever receive.

FAMOUS LAST WORDS

For Your Child

*"If I had my child to raise all over again,
I'd build self-esteem first and the house later.
I'd finger paint more and point the finger less.
I would do less correcting and more connecting.
I'd take my eyes off my watch and watch with my eyes.
I'd take more hikes and fly more kites.
I'd stop playing serious and seriously play.
I would run through more fields and gaze at more stars.
I'd do more hugging and less tugging."*
Diane Loomans – Speaker, Author & Coach

*"While we try to teach our children all about life,
our children teach us what life is all about."*
Angela Schwindt - Home schooling mum

For You

"Life is short and it is here to be lived."
Kate Winslet - Film Actress & Singer

*"Life is what happens while you
are busy making other plans."*
John Lennon - Singer/ Songwriter &
Co-Founder of the Beatles

*"Write it in your heart, that every day
is the best day in the year."*
Ralph Waldo Emerson - Essayist, Lecturer & Poet

ACKNOWLEDGEMENTS

Huge thanks to Michelle Lever for her beautiful illustrations.

© Copyright 'GROWN UP BOX OF TOYS' Library of Congress. Washington DC. 2008

Also available by Lorraine Michele

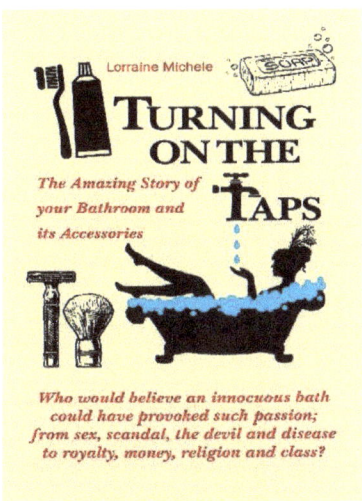

Turning On The Taps
The Amazing Story of your Bathroom and its Accessories

A thoroughly entertaining romp through history!

Who would believe an innocuous bath
could have provoked such passion;
from sex, scandal, the devil and disease,
to royalty, money, religion and class?

It may be the smallest room in the house....
but your bathroom will never be the same again.

Lightning Source UK Ltd.
Milton Keynes UK
UKHW020731290121
377850UK00007B/224